ONE UKRAINI
SUMMER

ONE UKRAINIAN SUMMER

A memoir about falling in love and coming of age in the former USSR

VIV GROSKOP

ITHAKA

First published by Ithaka Press
An imprint of Black & White Publishing Group
A Bonnier Books UK company

4th Floor, Victoria House,
Bloomsbury Square,
London, WC1B 4DA

Owned by Bonnier Books
Sveavägen 56, Stockholm, Sweden

Hardback – 978-1-80418-486-8
Ebook – 978-1-80418-487-5

A CIP catalogue of this book is available from the British Library.

Typeset by IDSUK (Data Connection) Ltd
Printed and bound by Clays Ltd, Elcograf S.p.A.

1 3 5 7 9 10 8 6 4 2

Ithaka Press is an imprint of Bonnier Books UK
www.bonnierbooks.co.uk

PEN International is a charity registered in England and Wales as International P.E.N. (Reg. No. 1117088).

Viv Groskop confirms that 100% of the income earned by her from this book will be donated to PEN International for their global work supporting writers at risk.

Find out more: www.pen-international.org

Author's Note

This is a memoir of the time I spent in the former Soviet Union in the early 1990s. The events in this book are true and the people are real. Names and some identifying details have been changed. These are my personal recollections of that time. Conversations are as I remember them. To write this book, I've relied on my memory and some personal notes. The translations and transliterations (transposing of the Cyrillic alphabet into English) are mine. Any linguistic errors or misunderstandings are mine. The language, spellings and references are intended to reflect my recollections of common post-Soviet usage in the early 1990s rather than the correct modern usage, particularly in reference to names and place names (i.e. Vladimir/Volodymyr, Kiev/Kyiv, Krivoy Rog/Kryvyi Rih. Odessa/Odesa).

In the dream, I see a flash of yellow through the train window. Look, Vivka. Sonyashniki. Sunflowers. *I can hear Roza's voice but I can't remember her face. My eyes are closed and I don't want to open them. Roza reaches up to the top bunk and pulls on the hem of my jeans where my feet are poking over the mattress. I'm not a tall person, but Soviet-issue train beds are not the longest and even someone as short as me is cramped. I think: how are you supposed to sleep on a train if you are tall, like a KGB agent? Although I suppose you don't have to be tall to be in the KGB. And maybe you wouldn't travel on a train if you were in the KGB anyway. You would travel in one of those special cars they call a Black Marusya. Or is that a prison truck? Why am I thinking about the KGB? The KGB doesn't need to be in this dream. Everyone keeps telling me the KGB doesn't exist any more anyway. Stop being obsessed with the KGB, Vivka. Eto po-staromy.* That is the old way.

My limbs are stiff and I've had enough of this train. Something is itching. Roza gasps and points out of the window. This time I see her face. She has pale little pixie features, a shock of dyed orange hair and John Lennon glasses that make her look like an old lady librarian. I'm 21, and I think everyone looks old. She is probably about 30. I scooch round on the top bunk and pull myself onto my elbows.

The scene flashing by the windows could be out of a film, a reel still on replay 30 years later. Endless sunflowers form a glorious blur of yellow against the blue of the sky, like a firestorm. They are almost gaudy, a scene from a tourist board promotion. If such a thing existed after the collapse of the Soviet travel company Intourist. Why am I thinking about Intourist? They don't exist any more either. Everyone says so. It's like a meteor shower of sunflowers, a blast of sunshine screaming, 'Welcome to Ukraine! You are no longer in Russia!' *Or maybe I am the one internally screaming that?*

In the dream, I blink the tiredness and the irritation out of my eyes. It has been a long journey. I want to breathe. I want to hear my own thoughts in the right language. What is the right language? Ya razmovlayu trozhki na ukrainskuyu movi. I speak a little Ukrainian. *I am tired of holding my breath and trying to understand. Roza is shouting at me on the train. She seems angry, but it's just because the noise from the tracks is so loud. I should be used to someone talking Russian so fast. But the train is noisy, and I am losing every other word. I put my book down. I am not reading it anyway; I am only half-pretending to read so that Roza will stop talking to me. Or rather, at me. She has talked at me all the way from Moscow to Kiev, a journey of 12 hours. A journey with no earplugs.*

The flash of yellow lights up both our faces and we laugh. I don't want to feel like a tourist, I don't want to be a cliché. But the sunflowers really are breathtaking. Roza is not an outsider and even she is moved by them.

She sits back down at the window, cups her chin in her hand and sighs with contentment. For once, I think we are having a moment of quiet companionship. Savour it.

I get it now. This is not a dream. This is real. It is a memory. I have been dreaming what I remember. Roza suddenly looks straight at me. Vivka, have you ever tried Bounty? What is it like? Is it really the taste of paradise?

to walk, vb.
ходить, khodit' (Russian)
ходити, khodyty (Ukrainian)

It was a verb of motion that finally made me realise that I could understand some Ukrainian, a language I had not officially learned at all. In both Russian and Ukrainian, verbs of motion govern movement from place to place – to walk, to go, to arrive, to fly. These words have multiple variants according to the sort of motion being undertaken, whether self-powered or aboard a vehicle; according to whether the motion is still going on or whether it's finished; and according to whether you are going somewhere and staying, or you are going and intending to come back again. You don't even want to think about using these verbs in the past tense because then you've got all kinds of other problems on your hands. It's all very confusing and requires grammar books to use multiple arrows pointing in different directions. Motion is exhausting in both Russian and Ukrainian.

In the run-up to that summer, I had spent months trying to get my Russian verbs of motion right only to find myself thinking I was saying, *Let's go!* as I boarded a bus, when I was actually saying, *Let us walk upon foot!* At first, I avoided mistakes by not using verbs at all: *Avtobus! Velikolepno! A bus! Excellent!* Then I got serious, stopped over-analysing it and started religiously copying which words Russian speakers used in which situations. Sometimes, though, a verb of motion clicked into place and you just knew whether it sounded right. You felt it by instinct, knew it in advance without jumping through all these logistical hoops. Jumping is not a verb of motion, by the way. Because you tend to do it on the spot and there's no motion involved. Good to know.

That's how it was when I instinctively understood the Ukrainian word for *walked* – *khodiv*. I heard it from Bogdan's mother, Lyuba. She spoke in her own version of Ukrainian, which she had spoken since childhood, combined with some Russian. Her language was called *surzhyk*, non-standard 'mixed' Russian-Ukrainian, a concept I only heard about years later. Perhaps this word was mentioned to me at the time and I forgot it. Or perhaps no one would have mentioned it, as it is arguably controversial. Some people claim *surzhyk* is a language in its own right. Others call it a dialect. Some see it as uneducated. I just saw it as the way she spoke, and I wanted to understand her so very much. Was that because there was an unspoken thought at the back of my mind: 'This woman could be my mother-in-law'? *Mozhe buti. Maybe.*

Surzhyk means literally 'with rye', and is also the name of a bread made with wheat and rye flour. In linguistic terms, it means a mix of several things: a hybrid of Russian, Ukrainian and its own words. Maybe Lyuba spoke with rye all the time. Or perhaps she only spoke *surzhyk* with me because she wanted to make her Ukrainian more understandable. But in any case, I understood what she was trying to say to me about how hard Bogdan had tried to find me when I first arrived in Ukraine that summer: *vin khodiv i khodiv i nakonetz priishov.* This was slightly incorrect Ukrainian designed for me to understand. In Russian the same phrase is: *on khodil i khodil i nakonetz prishol. Vin* is equivalent to *on* (he); *khodiv* is *khodil* (walked). It means *he walked and walked and at last he arrived.* Or *he walked and walked and at last he got to the end of his walk.* It shows two things: one, this verb of motion indicates that the 'going' was accomplished on foot; two, it's a brilliant illustration of the different form of the verb used according to whether the action is finished or not. So when his walking was continuing, one kind of verb is used, and when it is finished, another kind comes in. The walking had been completed. He had brought me home to her.

I couldn't have worked out how to say these things in Ukrainian myself. I had been learning Russian for almost three years at this point, and although the two languages are alike, they are not identical. When these things were said to me, however, they were close enough to the words I knew in Russian for me to understand. *Vin khodiv i khodiv* became something of a catchphrase with us – *he walked and he walked* – because it sounds funny and exhausting in Ukrainian, much more so, for some reason, than when you translate it into Russian. I can't even explain why this is. It just is.

Bogdan's mother was also very good at being extremely dramatic and demonstrative in her speaking, so her enactment of *vin khodiv i khodiv* was undertaken as if she were narrating a great fairy tale to a group of children: her eyes were wide, her forehead furrowed, her eyebrows moved up and down, her shoulders slumped with effort as she carefully showed the motion of 'walking to the point of completion' with her fingers crossing the palm of her hand. All in order that the stupid Russian-speaking foreigner could understand what she was trying to say. She acted out mopping her brow. It was a hot day for a long walk.

Of course, she wanted me to understand the words. But I also understood the meaning behind them, with or without rye: *He waited for you. And then when you arrived, he had no idea where you were. And he walked for miles to find you. He walked and walked.* She meant well, and her pantomime was good-natured. But there was a question behind it that didn't need spelling out in any language: *Who are you, to cause all this fuss?*

the previous year, adj. n.
в прошлом году, v proshlom godu (Russian)
в минулому році, v mynulomu rotsi (Ukrainian)

The first time I met him, the temperature was falling and I was madly in love. The second time I met him, it was starting to snow, and I got scared that I was *too* in love and tried to break it off. The third time I met him, it was -10C, and he promised me that if I could get through one Russian winter, he would make sure that we had one Ukrainian summer together, just the two of us. *Davai*, I replied, which is the same in Ukrainian and in Russian. *Go on, then*.

When we first met, the Neva – the river running through St Petersburg – was already starting to freeze into frothy high peaks. Before that long train journey through Ukraine with Roza during the summer of 1994, before *vin khodiv i khodiv*, before the sunflowers against the blue of the sky, before we ate watermelons in the street and corn on the cob on the beach, before we fell asleep on a veranda underneath a canopy of grape vines, before the sunset in Odessa, there was a Russian winter: the winter of 1993 into 1994, which would turn out to be one of the coldest for years.

Whether you were from that place or just visiting, it was a strange and disorientating moment, four years since the fall of the Berlin Wall. 'Soviet' was dead as an idea. People didn't even like to say the word any more. But they still talked about things being *sovkovy*: Soviet-ish. *Sovkovy* comes from the word *sovok* (dustpan). A Russian friend told me solemnly that it means 'from the times of the Soviet Union and bad quality'. I took it to mean 'rubbish in a Soviet way'. It was a time when everything was caught in the in-between. Nothing was quite Communist any more, but neither was it quite Westernised either – as if someone had started to sweep up the mess, but no one had emptied the dustpan. Russia and Ukraine were both located geographically inside a version of a country that didn't exist any more: the former Soviet Union. And most people were located psychologically inside a *sovkovy* mindset that was past its sell-by date.

It was seven years since a nuclear powerplant worker in Sweden first reported inexplicably high levels of radiation on his shoes 700 miles away from Ukraine, the first sign in the world outside the USSR of what was happening in the No. 4 reactor of the Chernobyl nuclear power plant. And it was eight years since I had first, at the age of 12, seen the video for Elton John's 'Nikita' ('Hey Nikita, is it cold in your little corner of the world?') and decided that I would very much like to study Russian at university.

This was a popular choice for swotty linguists in the late 1980s. There were plenty of reasons for a teenager from a small town in the West Country to be interested in this famously exotic, sprawling, mysterious place. Like Gorbachev being on television all the time with his birthmark and his smiley face. And Anna Karenina and

Chekhov and Chagall. And having a poster of a youthful Stalin on my bedroom wall from the days before he became a tyrannical despot (and from the days before I realised the poster was in very bad taste). For me, though, there was something else too: a personal connection. Somewhere at the back of my mind, I was drawn eastwards by trying to work out where my weird surname – Groskop – was really from. Genealogy websites were far in the future and the adults in my family had no satisfying answers to the many questions I had about our identity. Years later, the internet would be invented, a cousin in Canada would send us a family tree and I would learn that my name was Polish and Jewish, and had nothing to do with anything Russian. This was something which was probably already obvious to any person with even a vague understanding of Jewishness. But no one posed the question to my face until I was almost 30 – by which time it was too late, and I had already spent over a decade learning Russian, trying to 'rediscover my roots'.

All this was unknown to me then, and even the desire to trace my imaginary heritage was something faint and intangible. Mostly I was going to the former Soviet Union for the reasons anyone travels a long way from home in their teens or twenties: because I wanted to know who I was now that I was no longer a child. Because I wanted to be my own person separate from my family. Because I was curious. And because I was a nerd who wanted to learn the nerdiest language of them all.

I was also there out of necessity: in order to pass my university course, I had to spend a year abroad. I was studying French and Russian, and at the end of my first year I had almost failed Russian. I couldn't wimp out and just go to France for the year. I could not be defeated by this language. I needed to get to grips with it, no matter how tough it got. Which is how I found myself in October 1993 in a nightclub nearly 2000 miles from home, in a country which covered 11 of the world's 24 time zones, staring at a Ukrainian man whose handsomeness was of ludicrous proportions, a man who would turn out to be called literally 'God's Gift, son of God's Gift', and who would come to promise me the summer of my dreams on tour with him and his rock band, the one and only 'Ukraine answer to Red Hot Chili Pepper'.

*   *   *

When I met Bogdan, it was at the beginning of this compulsory year and the first time I had lived outside the UK for any significant length of time. But this wasn't my first time in Russia. There had been another summer – and another man, a Russian called Dima. Fortunately, Dima and I were just friends by the time I met Bogdan. But being just friends was enough to make things awkward and complicated, especially when knowing a foreigner at all was a valuable commodity and people were precious about sharing their newly acquired post-Communist assets.

I first met Dima the Russian when I spent a month in St Petersburg in 1992 taking an intensive language course, trying to reverse the horror of the near-failed exam. I was living with an Intourist-approved landlady, or *khozyaika*. This is what they called the women in the host families who took in foreign students. They were often elderly ladies who lived alone, and wanted to make a bit of extra money by allowing a foreigner to sleep in the bedroom of their two-room apartment while they were relegated to the sofa in the living room. It was my first encounter with the weirdness of the post-Soviet world.

This was in the city of St Petersburg, a new name for Leningrad that people were still getting used to and often forgot to use. The USSR had collapsed barely six months before and that August was bleak. It was obvious even to outsiders with very little understanding of the place that life was becoming surreal. The past was gone. And yet it seemed that nothing was being constructed in its place. Apart from kiosks: there were kiosks everywhere, on every corner, at every metro station, windows steamed up from the inside and packed with hundreds of varieties of imported cigarettes. People were both guarded and reckless at the same time, shy of connecting with Westerners but also desperately curious. There was a precarity to existence that our host families tried to shield us from. But we could see the queues both inside and outside the shops. And we could see that the kiosks never had queues. They were too expensive.

Outside the metro stations there would always be a few *babushki* selling pathetic, random items on upturned cardboard boxes: a saucepan, a cup, a biro. Selling something you owned for a few roubles could be the difference in whether you bought a loaf of bread that day or not. The average person spent an hour queuing daily just to get basic items. Most people were not exactly starving, although many were desperate and on edge. Pretty much everyone was resentful, exhausted and humiliated. There was a famous Soviet joke that dated back decades: 'We pretend to work and they pretend to pay us.' But when the music had stopped, even the pretending was over.

If you had family, neighbours, colleagues and a network then you usually found ingenious ways of making things last and getting by. The cost of living was no longer under state control and was wildly unpredictable. That year inflation reached 2000 per cent.

People hoarded both money and goods because they never knew when the currency would be devalued or when things would run out in the shops. The ownership of 'hard currency', illegal in the USSR, was a grey area, and you couldn't use foreign money to pay for anything publicly. Despite this, most people immediately converted their roubles to US dollars and hid them in a tin at home, because it was the only way the money would hold its value. Food was harder to stash. An urban kitchen would have a whole wall of hundreds of jars of pickled vegetables, food grown on allotments and on land at the *dacha* (summer house) outside town, the one thing you could rely on to keep through the winter. An apartment might have a glorious balcony with a view over the city, but no one ever went out onto it because it was being used as storage space for *ogurtsy* (salted gherkins).

That summer of 1992, war broke out in the semi-autonomous region of Abkhazia, on the eastern coast of the Black Sea. This was a long way away and had no immediate impact on life in St Petersburg, and yet it was a sign of something uncomfortable: it seemed unlikely that all the many regions and republics of the Soviet Union would transition into a new era without some kind of reckoning. The end of the USSR was supposed to have happened 'without a single shot being fired', as our university textbooks used to tell us. But how long could that last? People were jittery and superstitious. They had already begun to believe that bad things happened in the summer. The idea of 'the August curse' had taken root in people's minds the previous year. In August 1991, Gorbachev went on holiday to the Crimea. In his absence, a group of Communist hardliners in Moscow attempted a coup against him, protesting his progressive reforms. They meant to 'save' the USSR but their plan backfired and only hastened its demise as one by one the republics began to announce their independence, with Ukraine one of the first in line. Gorbachev had won. But the Union was lost.

By the time I first filled in a visa application, the economy had been in 'shock therapy' for half a year. The effect on the population would later be estimated as twice as intense as the Great Depression in Western Europe and the United States. State assets were changing hands without any planning, oversight or accountability, allowing a handful of people with connections and influence to take charge of whole industries like oil, gas, aluminium, banking. . . . Your fate depended on your network and on your willingness to take risks and bend the rules. If you knew someone who knew someone, and you had a deal to offer, then you had a chance of making a fortune, especially if you were lucky enough to have contacts in organised crime.

All of this was happening largely invisibly, as most people concentrated on surviving day to day, muttering darkly about *bandity* (bandits), which became a catch-all term for everyone from small-time thieves and black marketeers to politicians and the opportunistic businessmen – because they were all men – who would one day become known as oligarchs.

The unease was pervasive. But there was also relief, freedom and a sort of mild chaos. A lot of the Russians I met, including Dima, were funny, with a dry, dark sense of humour. Once you got past the outer layer of the public persona, in their own homes people were warm and welcoming, and couldn't do enough for you. This was one humiliation people were not prepared to live through: they kept face in front of foreigners by serving tea out of a samovar on their finest bone china, adding spoonfuls of homemade cranberry jam.

* * *

Everything was new to me that first Russian summer, and there were a lot of 'firsts'. First taste of black bread. First spoonful of caviar. First sip of Borjomi, the bitter Georgian mineral water everyone loved. The first time someone stepped out of a side street as if from nowhere to ask in Dickensian English, 'Please. Excuse me for the interruption. I would like Levi's jeans.' This was pronounced as one word and with 'Levi's' to rhyme with 'lettuce': levice-jeans. 'You can sell them to me?'

Then there was the first time you queued in a post office or a shop for up to an hour, only to get to the front of the queue and have the window slammed shut in your face; a sign would appear that said *technicheskii pereryv* (technical break). I would always think, 'It is not "technically a break" if you've shut up shop. There's nothing technical about it. It's an actual break. Just call it a break.' And the first time someone poured you what was supposed to be a shot of vodka, but you realised that they were pouring the liquid into what was really quite a large water glass and − oh, right, I see − they were going to fill it to the brim and expect you to down it in one otherwise you would be insulting their family. *Obidno. Pei do dna. You are insulting me. Drink up.* This was a word I would hear constantly: *Obidno.* It means: *it is insulting. It is offensive. It is hurtful.* People were easily insulted.

I was not exactly surprised by what I encountered on that first visit. The queues and the disintegration were well documented on

TV back home. But the reality of it was overwhelming, suffocating and guilt-inducing. I was always on the lookout for people who were gentle and patient, who could help me to navigate the weirdness. Fortunately, I had landed with Elizaveta Dmitrievna, my host mother. She thought Viv was a silly name, and instead began to call me VIP (Veep or Vipulya for the affectionate form). She thought that VIP (Very Important Person) suited me better. Soon, everyone called me Vipulya: teeny tiny little VIP.

But much as I wanted to connect with Elizaveta Dmitrievna, I was of course only there because my Russian was actively bad, and initially we had immense communication difficulties. We couldn't maintain a conversation for longer than about 20 minutes – although that was in itself an achievement, since I could barely get past 'hello' with a lot of Russians. The eventual gains I made with Elizaveta Dmitrievna were largely down to the fact that she had spent most of her working life as a qualified teacher of the deaf, and so was proficient in what I assumed were various different forms of sign language. As a result of this, it was much easier to communicate with her than with most people. She was very good at acting out words and thinking of how to say something creatively without using language. For years afterwards, I would find myself finally hearing, learning and understanding Russian phrases that she had tried patiently to sound out to me and help me get, using extravagant hand pictures and signals.

One morning, Elizaveta Dmitrievna proudly served me a single tomato on a plate for breakfast. Fresh tomatoes were a rare treat, and this was a big deal. I didn't want to eat it. It was too precious. I tried to protest. In order to change the subject, she spent almost an hour trying to ask me something that I would only realise much later was a very simple question: 'Vipulya, what did you see in your sleep?' The phrase 'What did you see in your sleep?' simply means, 'Did you have a dream last night?' I did not know this at the time. Her pantomime skills were beautiful. She would close her eyes and mumble as if talking in her sleep, while her hands drew pictures around her head. I could understand her saying, 'What did you see . . .?', so I kept saying, 'What did I see where?' We shouted at each other at cross purposes for a while, with her acting out a person opening their eyes and yawning. It didn't help to resolve my confusion that the expression *in your sleep* – *vo snye*, a phrase I didn't know – sounded to me like the word for *snow* – *snyeg*, a word I *did* know – and I couldn't understand why she kept asking me about what I could see in the snow. Eventually, we gave up and moved on to an even more futile conversation about sharing the solitary tomato, even though I knew how that would play out: I would try to give her half of the tomato and she would refuse. *Vipulya, ty zhe VIP. Delit'sya ne nado. Obidno. You are a VIP, Vipulya. It is not necessary to share. You are insulting me.*

* * *

It was while I was living with Elizaveta Dmitrievna that I met Dima. He was good-looking and loud, and his family didn't have any connections to Intourist, the official crumbling state travel programme. There was a whole network of people still catering for all the foreign visitors in the post-Soviet vacuum. Dima was not part of that system, which was mostly made up of people who worked for state-run educational institutions. He just happened to be a school friend of the son of one of our host families. Much as I appreciated the kindness of Elizaveta Dmitrievna, she was a pensioner, and I was desperate to make friends with Russians of my own age. I gravitated towards Dima as a 'real person' – not someone put in front of me by the state apparatus, someone who was my age, someone fun. Thanks to Dima, by the time I left at the end of August, my Russian was on track, and I had a whole gang of friends who had taken me to parties, made me try Belomorkanal cigarettes, Red October chocolate and Eskimo ice cream, and who didn't feel *sovkovy* or as if they were part of the system. They felt the same as my friends back home, even though realistically we didn't have much more in common than our age and the fact that we were all extravagantly committed smokers.

My status with Dima was unclear from the start. We sort of dated casually on and off. I stayed with his family when I went back again to visit in December 1992, bringing a job lot of his favourite Iron Maiden T-shirts with me. It was on that visit that I realised Dima already had a girlfriend, and suddenly the parameters of our relationship came sharply into view. Her name was Valentina – the perfect Valentine – and she had cute, doll-like features. She was a very serious girlfriend in every sense. When I was introduced to her, I understood what their relationship was just by looking at her eager, heart-shaped face. The words for *friend, boyfriend, acquaintance* and *fiancé* are complicated – and loaded – in Russian. There are a lot of options to choose from. When Valentina talked about Dima, she used the word *zhenikh*, the one that came closest to *fiancé*, even though – as far as I knew (although what did I know?) – they were not technically engaged to be married. It was a word that was sometimes used ironically or jokingly. But not in this case. They looked as if they belonged together.

In our group of friends everyone had glossed over whether Dima and I were just mates or something more. Now I saw why. From the first day I had known him, he had been intense and over the top, but also flaky and distracted. He was handsome and charismatic, tall and angular with big lips of a young Mick Jagger and the arrogance to match. He had a temper, and was prone to sulking. I was not going to fight anyone for him. And I wasn't serious enough about him to be angry either. He thought I was making a big deal about nothing and that there was no need to draw a line. *Obidno. Kakaya tebe raznitsa? It's insulting. What difference does it make to you?* But I wasn't about to muscle in on someone else's *zhenikh.*

I wasn't impressed with Dima's behaviour, and he could be a pain, but we still got on well. Added to that was the problem that if I had broken off from him completely, I would not have known anyone in St Petersburg, the city in which I was planning to spend a whole year. I made it clear that he needed to be faithful to his girlfriend and that we should be friends only. He just had to accept it. *Yesli ty s nei, ty ne so mnoi. If you are with her, you are not with me.*

And so it was that Dima and I continued an uneasy friendship. We were no longer in a romantic relationship. And I became good friends with his girlfriend and his family. At one point he even visited me in England, and stayed with my family in the south-west for a couple of weeks. We were doing a reasonable job of keeping things platonic, I thought. While he was in England, he had to visit the GP to get some antibiotics for a chest infection. The receptionist physically swooned when she saw him and said, 'Viv! He's like a film star!' I rolled my eyes.

By the time I arrived for the whole year, in September 1993, it was still awkward with Dima. I was tied to him in some way because he was the main person I knew. But I wasn't about to forget that he had started a relationship with me when he was already with someone else. In turn, he was annoyed with me for having broken off the relationship over what he regarded as the minor detail of him having a girlfriend.

We did not trust each other. I continued our 'friendship' thinking that he would become more normal over time. And he continued our 'friendship' thinking that I would eventually see sense and go back to being his (secondary) girlfriend. Looking back, I suspect there were also other women in this arrangement-that-I-had-not-signed-up-for, who neither I nor Valentina knew about. I began to realise that he was still waiting for me to give in to what he saw as the inevitable, and that maybe trying to be friends was a bad idea.

Unfortunately, by the time I caught on to this, a series of unforeseen events meant that I was already living in a two-room flat with Dima and his entire family.

autumn, n.
осень, osen' (Russian)
осінь, osin' (Ukrainian)

It was during that October that I met Bogdan. He was idly tapping out a drum beat on the table with a soft pack of Apollo-Soyuz cigarettes. It was not the same drum beat that was coming from the speakers in the club – he was in his own little world. Not only was he the most beautiful man I had ever seen, he had the superhuman ability to tune out Ace of Base. Their hit single 'All That She Wants (Is Another Baby)' had been on a loop everywhere since our group of British students had first arrived in the city more than a month before. I had translated the lyric 'She's the hunter, you're the fox' about 47 times already, while trying to explain that there was no intrinsic deeper meaning to the song and, no, I did not think that *mozhet ana beremennaya v pesnye, she might be pregnant in the song*, although that interpretation is theoretically possible, and who can read the minds of these Swedish musical geniuses? Maybe she really is literally desirous of birthing a second child and that is the message of this inimitable piece of music.

I hung out at Kosmos, this nightclub, a couple of evenings a week. Like many businesses in those days, there was no clear economic rationale to its existence. In theory it had an elastic and unpredictable door policy, brilliantly known in made-up English as *face control* (pronounced aggressively, *feis kontrol*). In reality, most of the time no one seemed to be in charge. The opening hours were random, and so was the pricing and availability of drinks. The only people who went there were kids in their late teens connected to the place in some way. Either their friends were playing in a band, or they knew someone who worked there. I went there to drink the local beer, Baltika, to smoke too many cigarettes with British friends who were also starting their year in Russia, and to get away from Dima: these musos were not his people, and I had managed to keep him away from this place. Some of us Brits had elected to spend the compulsory year abroad teaching English to Russian adults, and were working at the Vatson (Watson) School of English around the corner from Kosmos. The Vatson School of English was not connected to anyone called Watson. It was so called because Watson (or, more accurately, Vatson) was a name Russians could pronounce, and with which they had positive associations thanks to Sherlock Holmes. It was a name that inspired in Russians a feeling of all in this world that is cosy, comforting and English. For our Russian students, the best thing about the Vatson School of English was that it felt authentic. For us, their British teachers, the best thing about the Vatson School of English was that it was near a nightclub which – most of the time – sold cheap beer.

We had found out about Kosmos through young Russians connected to our host families. One of them was in a band called Oedipov Komplex which is, unsurprisingly, Russian for Oedipus Complex. They styled themselves like A Flock of Seagulls: bowl haircuts, New Romantic fringes, mohair jumpers, drainpipe trousers. The guys in the band were sweet and friendly, and spoke more English than most. They were very excited about the name of their band. They were even more excited to have a coterie of potential British groupies, not least because after many long years of waiting behind the Iron Curtain, they finally had access to people who could give them information about the greatest rock bands of all time.

They asked us earnestly about groups we were only vaguely aware of: rock legends of the 1970s like King Crimson, Uriah Heep, Deep Purple. They spoke of these people with reverence and pained, passionate intensity. Their hope was palpable: they wanted to commune deeply with us about the great artistry of this music. They would sing, hum, murmur at us, perhaps a good-natured riff from Peter Gabriel's 'Solsbury Hill': 'Saturday, I've come to take you home.' The lyric was actually 'Grab your things, I've come to take you home,' but that was too complicated.

We responded to enquiries about these ancient bands with blank looks. It was the only time I wished I had brought my dad with me to a nightclub. He probably knew some trivia about Led Zeppelin. The faces of Oedipov Komplex fell, and their hairsprayed fringes quivered with disappointment as they realised we had no intel on Jethro Tull or Robert Fripp. *A kak zhe tak? But how can this be. . .?* At home in England people were either listening to Radiohead or Take That. *A eto kto? Ne slyshal. Who the hell are they? Never heard of them.* It turned out that they had also never heard of A Flock of

Seagulls and had copied their look only accidentally. The hairstyles were just intended to annoy their parents. And their trousers were too tight, I later realised, mostly because they each only had one pair and had long outgrown them.

*   *   *

Like many public places – shops, businesses, schools – Kosmos barely advertised itself and you had to know it was there. There was no signage besides a small silver plaque bearing a Star Trek-type picture of a planet, on the exterior of the building. From the outside you'd think it was an office. Maybe Mr Spock's office. This anonymity applied to many things during the post-Soviet era, both literally and metaphorically. Something might exist in theory or even in reality but it didn't mean you needed to tell everyone about it. The right people would just know. It was confusing, but also a pleasant surprise when you're used to the consumerist opposite, the bling and branding that signal an invitation: 'Come and buy things in here! Come in and spend money!' In places where capitalism rules, you are welcome everywhere because it is understood that you are intending to buy stuff. In the places where capitalism was illegal and no one had any money, it was understood you were not really welcome anywhere, so you had better make your own fun.

Capitalism was permitted now, theoretically speaking. It was no longer illegal to run a private business. But it was the early days of the post-Soviet era and the hierarchy between state and private was blurred. This was not surprising as no one had been allowed to run anything commercially for the best part of seven decades. But it meant that most establishments operated in a grey area: you might find yourself in a state building in which some people were still paid by the state, but someone inside that building might also be importing some stuff from Germany and selling it off. It was best not to ask too many questions, as in any case no one could really explain who was doing what or how.

Inside, Kosmos was strangely, incongruously glamorous: over the top, frothy and kitsch. It was shabby but clean, and the interiors were like something out of another era: Art Deco light fittings, deep red carpets, velvet banquettes. It must have been some kind of state-run cabaret joint in the Soviet years, or maybe a wedding venue. Back home in England the year before, everyone had been watching the TV show *Twin Peaks*, and this place reminded me of it: smoke curling upwards, drapes everywhere, pockets of darkness, and a stage with a drum kit and a spotlight. The place was dimly lit and gave the impression of being magical, even though you knew that if anyone turned the lights on, it would be seedy and depressing.

Next to the dance floor was a long table where we would sit and smoke. The table was never full usually, but the night I met Bogdan it was hard to find a seat. I was wearing the kind of clothes that were designed to help me survive the plummeting temperatures: heavy trousers and big knits. Not what I would have worn to a nightclub back home. My corduroy thighs were a tight squeeze under the table. I pulled slightly at the neck of my Aran cardigan. Was I going to be too hot? I lit a Marlboro Light. I was in a strange mood that night. The last month had been a trial. I had started to doubt my decision to spend a year in this weird place. But I was also excited. It was still very early in the academic year, even if it had got off to a bad start, and even if Dima was the flatmate from hell. I had only really begun to hang out in this club to get away from him. That night I was planning to get lost in the chat of the group and smoke a lot.

When I looked up and saw Bogdan's face across the table for the first time, I almost burst out laughing. He was so exceptionally good-looking that it was actually funny. I studied him for a bit and then said aloud in English to anyone who could hear, 'I am sitting opposite a god.' I suppose I ought to have been more discreet. But first, it was true. And second, no one really understood anything you said in English unless you spelled it out several times – sometimes eventually having to write it down or get a dictionary out.

In any case, at this time in my life – actually, generally in my life – I had no game plan with relationships. Usually if I liked someone, I just told them. It exposed you to rejection very early, but it also saved a lot of time and messing about. And even if he didn't like me – and why should he, with my Aran cardigan knitted by my grandmother, my pasty English face and my total lack of knowledge about the back catalogue of Genesis and Yes? – well, he might as well enjoy knowing that a total stranger thought he was godlike.

It transpired that the beautiful man was there with two of his bandmates, Borys, the bass guitarist, and Artem, the singer. There was a drummer too, but everyone ignored him, and he sat on his own drinking at the bar. Borys was charismatic, loud and excitable. He explained energetically in a mixture of Russian, Ukrainian and heavily disguised English that their band was called Colney Hatch. Or as he pronounced it, Kolni Khetch. Borys waited expectantly for my impressed reaction and pulled his head back quizzically when there was none. *Patzany, ana Colney Hatch ne znaet. Lads, she doesn't know what Colney Hatch is.* Artem, the singer, came over and they started arguing. They had chosen this name on purpose. And they sang intentionally in English – not in Russian or in Ukrainian – for a reason: to connect with English-speaking audiences. Now they were coming face-to-face with real-life English speakers and Kolni Khetch meant nothing. This was a problem.

Artem, who immediately seemed gentler and less in-your-face than Borys, explained patiently that they had named their band after the famous first *sumasshedshiy dom* in England: the first mental asylum. Again, they waited for me to say 'Wow.' But there was really nothing I could say in reaction to this. I was thinking, 'Surely they mean Bedlam? Shall I tell them about Bedlam?' I knew they would not want to hear this and that I would not be able to explain Bedlam in any language, so I kept my mouth shut. In fact, Bedlam had existed since the 1400s. But there was also a 19th-century asylum, the largest in Europe, eventually known as Friern Hospital, in the London borough of Barnet, and it *was* originally called Colney Hatch Lunatic Asylum. In 1993, however, there was no Google to settle this question, so I let it lie.

It is not difficult to guess what they said when I asked, *A pochemu takoe imya? Why call yourselves that?* Artem smiled, stuck his tongue out and said something in English that was as terrible as it was predictable: 'Because we are crazy!' Well, I walked into that. Crazy guys, crazy band name. Moving things along, I asked, *A muzyka kakaya? What kind of music do you play?* This they answered very proudly, puffing their chests up: 'We are Ukraine answer to Red Hot Chili Pepper.' At least they had modelled themselves on a band that had been prominent in the UK in the last ten years. It was an improvement on Deep Purple.

I was politely impressed, correcting them with mild passive aggression, deliberately enunciating the definite article and the plural of pepper, seeing as I was working as an English teacher: *Ukraine's answer* to *the Red Hot Chilli Peppers. Ponyatno, I see. Nichevo sebe, good on you.* They had been playing some gigs in St Petersburg and this was their last weekend in town. They came here regularly and also spent time in Moscow. They couldn't get many gigs in Ukraine. *Infrastructury nema. There is no infrastructure.* I could understand what they were saying but they often used words that didn't exist in Russian like *nema* (there isn't any). I didn't know this was Ukrainian. I had no idea what Ukrainian was.

The beautiful man had so far said nothing and kept looking at the table and fidgeting with his cigarette packet as his friends tap-danced, trying to impress me. It was Borys, the bass guitarist, who noticed how I was looking at Bogdan, and who engineered it so that we were pushed together. I asked the beautiful man, 'What's your name?' He mumbled an answer and I frowned as I couldn't understand a word of it. Borys repeated the name clearly. I took a moment to understand it. And then could not stop laughing. Bogdan Bogdanovich. Gift of God, son of Gift of God. In Russian, *Bog* means *God*; the verb *dat'* is *to give*; in Ukrainian, *Boh* and *davati*. Or, if you prefer: *He who is God-given.* In any language, this man was a walking literal translation. I did not know how to say *Thank God* in Ukrainian at that time. But I would soon learn it: *Dyakuyu, Bohovi.*

*   *   *

It was most unfortunate that on the morning of the day of our first meeting I had woken up with a familiar tingle on my lip. I knew it to be the beginnings of a cold sore of hideous, humungous proportions – the curse of the herpes simplex virus, HSV-1, probably caused by the extreme drop in temperature that had come with the early onset of winter. That or stress. Because I was quite stressed.

My condition was definitely not to be confused with HSV-2, the cause of genital herpes. This kind of cold sore was known in Russian as *prostoy herpes* (simple herpes). As opposed to the complicated, promiscuous one. But still, it was the sort of cold sore that makes you think you had better stay at home. Definitely the sort of cold sore you don't want if you are about to meet someone who you dream will fall in love with you, someone you would like to kiss. And especially not if this someone is the sort of person who looks as if they just walked off the set of a rock video, accompanied everywhere by a wind machine. I knew this guy was in a band – we went to the nightclub especially to hang out with the guys who were in bands – and, sure, I wanted to be his groupie, and, yes, I believed in signs from the universe. But this was ridiculous. 'Hey! You're in a band. I want to be your groupie and I have arrived with ready-made herpes.'

I had seriously considered not going out that night at all because of the cold sore. But given the choice between going out with simple herpes emblazoned across my face and staying in with Dima glowering at me from the sofa. . . Well, it was an easy choice. Looking across the table, even if my lower face was throbbing slightly, I sensed it was the right one. Bogdan was shy and quiet, and looked down a lot. He was quick to laugh, easy-going, even-tempered. He looked Italian to me, mostly because at that time I had no reference points for the place he was from. Green eyes with flecks of gold, long eyelashes, tanned olive skin, long tawny hair. He had a cigarette permanently in his hand. He almost always wore what he was wearing the first time I saw him: double denim – dark jeans, a lighter blue denim for the jacket – with a grey polo neck underneath.

It wasn't that he was cool – although he *was* cool. The thing you simply could not fail to notice about him was that he was just – *just!* – beautiful. Perfect, even. He was 23 and I had just turned 20.

That first night of meeting Bogdan, it was clear that there was something between us from the start. But it was also clear it would definitely be me making the running. For the rest of the night Borys talked mostly on Bogdan's behalf. Bogdan definitely did not know that he was Gift of God, son of Gift of God. When it was obvious that people were going to stay at the club into the early hours, I got him to leave with me. How? I don't really know how. I think I just looked at him and said, *Poshli. Let's go by walking.* For once an accurate verb of motion, as it was past the time that public transport was running, and going on foot was the only possible option.

It was only when we got outside that he said, *Kuda? To where?* It was a usual thing for girls or young women to expect young men to walk them home, whether they knew them very well or not. It was the safest way to get home. I think he thought that was what I was asking. Unfortunately for him, that was not what I was asking.

We left around midnight and started to walk in a circle around Sennaya, the big open market space near Kosmos. This had once been Dostoevsky's patch. Every few steps, Bogdan would pull me towards him and try ineffectually to wrap me in his fleece-lined denim jacket – not as a romantic thing, just a precaution against hypothermia. He was staying round the corner from the club so we got bottles of beer from somewhere – a kiosk? Where else? – and took them back to the place where he was staying, which turned out to be incredibly weird.

It was a 'hostel' even more horrible than the cockroach-ridden place I had been living in the previous month. The walls were peeling with queasy peppermint-coloured paint and the beds were covered in old blankets. It was as if it had once been a prison. The Ukrainians had said they had named themselves after an asylum, and now I felt as if I were in one. I tried to ask what kind of place this was. *Kommunalka.* Bogdan shrugged.

Communal flats were usually fairly large apartments, where you might have a couple of rooms to yourself, but you shared an entrance hall and a large communal kitchen. They had a bad reputation because you couldn't choose who you lived with. People often had terrible fallings-out with their neighbours, and a fight might break out if you put your wooden spoon on someone else's portion of the worktop. But I liked *kommunalki*: you had more space, more room to breathe. This place was not a *kommunalka*. It was a derelict hostel.

Still, we settled in. This was at a time of life where you drank until either the alcohol ran out or you fell asleep, and you talked until either the words ran out or you fell asleep. So we sat on the floor and drank and talked. Or rather, I talked. Bogdan didn't know what to make of me. I tried to talk to him about music, even though my knowledge of the Red Hot Chili Peppers began and ended with the song 'Under the Bridge'. I suddenly remembered that they had been photographed naked with socks on their penises. I struggled to voice this observation in Russian. 'They were naked. With socks. And some penis.' He laughed.

I wanted to make him laugh. And I wanted to make him look at me. I was so impatient in these situations. You like me or you don't like me. Just let me know, so we can get the rejection out of the way. I needed him to look at me so that I could tell either way. But not to look at me too closely. The cold sore was still tingling.

That first night, we did not sleep with each other, but we did sleep next to each other fully clothed, holding hands. For whatever reason — stupidity, naivety, youth or beer — it did not occur to me to think that this was not a safe place to stay. We lay down on one of the creepy blanketed prison beds, pulled our coats over us, looked at the cracked ceiling and fell asleep. It did not occur to me that I had a class to teach the next morning at which 20 hopeful adult learners would be waiting for me, dressed in kipper ties and corduroy jackets. I let myself fall asleep in this pistachio prison with a man, the most beautiful man in the world, whom I had just met and who had very little to say to me.

I sat bolt upright when I awoke, still holding hands with an extremely handsome Ukrainian. When I checked my Swatch (always the subject of great fascination and many questions), it was around 7am. Miraculously, I hadn't overslept and missed work. In the cold light of the dawn, I realised that the place was worse than I thought. It was more like a squat than a *kommunalka*, and it seemed as if it had been abandoned. There were piles of old furniture everywhere, and the toilets had cracked cisterns with no doors. I hovered over one of them to pee while humming loudly, rushed to wash my face in a broken sink with a cracked mirror, found some chewing gum in my pocket, and tried to make myself presentable by clawing my fingers through my hair. I needed to be at work by 7:30am. At least the Vatson School of English was nearby.

I woke Bogdan up. As he opened his eyes, he looked at me with no surprise, as if we were both meant to be there. 'I need to go to work.' *Zachem? What for?* This was the first of hundreds of times I would hear him say *Zachem?* A *sovkovy* type of word. *Why bother?* But he could see I could very much be bothered. I was ready to go.

He insisted on walking me halfway there. I didn't know what to say or how to say it. The things I would have said in English were clichés, like, 'When will I see you again?' But at least the things I could say in Russian were genuine: 'I like you.' Although embarrassingly, in Russian this is, 'You are pleasing to me.' I forced myself to say it. He looked suitably embarrassed. I wanted to be able to say something funny like, 'We must stop meeting like this.' But I didn't know how to say this. I only knew how to be unintentionally funny by saying things like, 'With socks and some penis.'

But the one good thing about Russian is that you can say, 'We'll see each other?' in a way that sounds non-committal and casual. *Uvidemsya?* I asked. He nodded. *Uvidemsya. We'll see each other.* I wrote the phone number of Dima's flat on a scrap of paper. We still hadn't kissed, and we were about to say goodbye. I remembered about the cold sore. I pointed to it, on one side of my mouth. I thought about saying, *Prostoy herpes, simple herpes*, but decided against it. Instead, I pointed to the other side of my mouth, as if to say, 'This is where you can kiss me.' He laughed. We both held one side of our lips together in a lop-sided half-smooch for long enough that it wasn't awkward any more. *Chuchelo*, he laughed. *Ty prosto chuchelo*. I didn't know what that meant.

I watched him walk away down the side of the canal back towards Sennaya in the morning mist. I didn't really care about anything except how I felt right at that moment: dizzyingly, madly, stupidly in love.

*   *   *

I didn't think much about where Bogdan came from or what that place might be like. Apart from Chernobyl and 'chicken Kiev',

I had no reference points for Ukraine. Bogdan and the boys in the band were the first Ukrainians I ever met. My teachers at university all identified as Russian or at least as Soviet émigrés. That was if anyone thought about identity or nationality at all at that time, which we didn't. Despite the fact that we were devoted to the study of the language of a monumentally gigantic country – albeit a recently deceased one, the former Soviet Union – with 286 million people, a land mass of 8.6 million square miles and a total of 15 republics (the Ukrainian Soviet Socialist Republic being the second largest after Russia), and despite the fact that we were supposed to be getting the most superior education on the planet (it was the University of Cambridge), it didn't seem to occur to anyone to wonder if perhaps this land mass, this people, this history could be broken down into separate components. Understanding it as a whole was difficult enough. Breaking it apart – even intellectually, let alone politically or geographically – was not something anyone had been keen to undertake.

People who studied this area – which we came to call 'The Region' – did not study, say, Ukrainian history; or if they did, I never encountered these people. They mostly studied the USSR and they called themselves Sovietologists. Or they studied Tolstoy and tried their best to ignore the existence of the USSR. Or they were eccentrics, like the people who studied Old Church Slavonic, the liturgical language of the Russian Orthodox Church between the ninth and the twelfth centuries. There was a module on Old Church Slavonic on my undergraduate degree course. There was no module for Ukrainian. I didn't even know it was a language. Even the people who were supposed to care about The Region more than anyone did not care about such things.

When I had first signed up to study Russian in the autumn of 1990, the Soviet Union still existed as an entity. By the time I actually started my first university term in October 1991 and began learning the Russian alphabet, the USSR was dead. I might have been learning a language spoken by almost 300 million people. But I was also learning the language of a country that no longer existed. It was a development that was in some ways completely inevitable and in others profoundly shocking. Many of the teachers and academics I knew at the time had been preparing for this moment for decades. One of my lecturers had been a translator for Gorbachev. Others were deeply enmeshed in the dissident movement. The Russians I knew were profoundly anglicised, having lived in the UK for years, rarely travelling back to what was really no longer 'home'. But what no one talked about or really acknowledged was this: What do you do if you are an expert in something that has vanished? And do you really know anything about what might come in its place?

Had I thought about Ukraine – or 'the Ukraine' as people called it then – before I met Bogdan and the other Ukrainians that night in Kosmos? Unlikely. Did I have any concept of what Ukraine was? No. Did I understand the differences between Russia and Ukraine? Definitely not. The distinction was academic at the time. People were still reminding themselves to say St Petersburg instead of Leningrad, to say Commonwealth of Independent States instead of USSR. (Weird how CIS never caught on, even 30 years later. It still exists, although obviously 'the Ukraine' has long since left it.) These boundaries and distinctions were fluid things that no one cared that much about. At that time if you had asked any of us to rate the chances of Russia waging war against Ukraine, we wouldn't even have understood the question. This was when very few people cared about the individual countries of this extinct Union, neither *zdes* (here, the former USSR) nor *tam* (over there, the West). Hardly anybody *tam* even understood where Chernobyl was (60 miles north of Kiev, 500 miles south-west of Moscow). When people from *zdes* asked me about England they always called it *tam*: 'What is the average monthly salary *tam*, Over There?' 'Does everyone drink Coca Cola *tam*, Over There?' 'What is it really like *tam*, Over There?' *Tam* was the magical Other for them. Sometimes they asked, disbelievingly, *A ty deistvitelno ottuda? Are you really from Over There?* They would check with their friends that I wasn't secretly Latvian or Lithuanian and trying to make a fool out of them. Of course for me, *zdes*, here, was the magical Other. And now there was only Here. And there was only Him, God's Gift.

* * *

It was true that I was besottedly in love. Or possibly in lust. But the other truth was this: by the time of my first meeting with Bodya, which was what everyone called God's Gift – Little Bogdan – I was subconsciously looking for a life raft. I had hoped to be settled by now, to feel at home in this city. Instead, I was tired and hungover most of the time, living on cigarettes, badly brewed bitter Turkish coffee and the adrenaline that comes from not understanding what people are saying to you 97 per cent of the time while still trying to argue with them and assert yourself. A month had passed, but it felt like a year. How was I going to stick it out? Worse, the Marlboro Lights were running out: I had brought a multi-pack from England, but supplies were dwindling. And while I had seen Marlboro Reds and Marlboro Menthols in kiosk windows, I had not seen the familiar

44

gold Lights packs anywhere. It would be a sorry day indeed if I was going to have to resort to Marlboro Menthols.

In order to get to work on time, I was getting up while it was not yet light, tiptoeing around the other three people in the two-room apartment. Katya, Dima's mother, slept in one bed with her 11-year-old daughter Inessa. I slept in another bed in the same room. Dima slept in the sitting room on the sofa bed. Dima was a legendarily heavy sleeper. You could have parked a Lada on his head and he wouldn't wake up. But still, it was the principle. Because if you did wake him up, he would kill you. No, really: he would kill you.

Invariably Katya would already have got up silently and would be waiting for me in the kitchen, fussing over me and whispering, '*Tikho, tikho,*' (quietly, quietly) as she made me coffee and ceremoniously placed a boiled egg in front of me. I tried so many times to tell her not to get up to make me breakfast and she would just say, *Tikho, tikho*. The boiled eggs were also a bone of contention. They were in short supply, and I knew I was only getting them because I was a foreigner. It was Elizaveta Dmitrievna's Tomato of Doom all over again. I implored Katya to stop buying eggs. I could never work out how to say things in a way that meant people would listen to me, while not being rude. In Russian, people do not say things like, 'You really don't need to . . .', or, 'I really don't mind if . . .'. And I didn't know how to get around that. *Yaitsy, ne nado. The eggs are unnecessary*.

Katya was an exceptionally beautiful and poised woman, and I adored her. She had puffy, Pre-Raphaelite blonde hair meticulously brushed into place and an angelic, gentle face. I had only seen her with her husband a few times. He was a naval captain and away at sea for months on end. I was young and stupid and knew nothing about what it took to keep a marriage going, but even I could see that everyone was more relaxed when he was not around. As far as I knew, he had not been at home for a few months now, and the mood in the flat was calm – more or less. Each morning, I would drink half of the coffee and eat as much as I could manage of the precious egg, Katya tutting and frowning kindly all the while. My actions were wasteful, but she was a benevolent feeder. She would walk me to the front door and see me off, kissing my head. She smiled. *Chastlivo, krasavitsa*, she said. *Go on the happy path, beautiful one*. I was desperate to go on the happy path.

I had moved into their place last-minute, lugging my one suit-case of stuff. The initial plan was not that I would be living with Dima's family – it had happened by accident. After two weeks in a hostel, where we had our teacher training, we were moved into host families. I was sent, as planned, to live with a family I didn't know, chosen by the school that had hired us to teach English. This was where we were supposed to spend the entirety of the next year. We would teach English to our classes, and the fees for this work would be paid directly to our host families for our board and lodging. In addition, as part of the deal we were supposed to teach English to our host families. And somehow, by osmosis, we would also learn Russian.

Even before this whole arrangement began to unravel, I struggled to understand how all this was going to pay for itself. The money side of things made me uneasy, and I worried about it a lot at that time. This was another student year for me, and I had a grant, so I had enough – but only as long as I stuck to what was planned. I also knew that what money I did have, which had to last the year, was a lot in post-Soviet terms. Even five pounds was a lot then: it could pay for food for more than a week. Still, you never knew quite what your money was worth. I was always moving between pounds, dollars and roubles in my mind. The exchange rate fluctuated so dramatically from one day to the next that you could end up losing a big chunk of your cash. When I first arrived the exchange rate was around 1000 roubles to the dollar. By the time I left a year later, it was closer to 3000. This was why I only changed five or ten dollars into roubles at a time.

There was a vast gulf between what a decent sum of money was to Russians and what one was to us. There was a dual pricing system everywhere, based on getting wealthy tourists to drop as much hard currency as possible on their three-day Intourist visits. A ticket to the opera could be up to £100 for foreigners, and 50p for Russians. Museums cost £15 for foreigners and 5p for Russians. If you tried to buy tickets anywhere and your Russian (and matching strident manner) was not flawless, you would be asked to show your passport and be charged the foreigner price.

As a student, I felt a strong pull to the Russian pricing system rather than to the foreigner rates. It was my dream to pay 5p to get into a museum. But I was also aware that I was excessively privileged in relation to almost everyone around me. The situation with the board and lodging and teaching made me uneasy because the sums of money changing hands were not made transparent. I was supposed to subsist on this quid pro quo arrangement: teach English – cluelessly and without any experience – to some random people, and we will feed you and give you a roof over your head. It had seemed like a good idea when I signed up for it, but now I was in the thick of it I didn't like it at all. There was no way I was going to teach English in class five days a week and then get bugged at 'home' for more English teaching. My sole purpose, my absolute sole and obsessive purpose, that year was to learn to speak Russian and not fail any more exams. I didn't see how speaking English in the place where I was living would help me with that.

Worse, my host family did not feel like 'home'. It was excruciating. They were a mother and daughter, and I had to call the mother by her formal name, Maria Alexandrovna (Maria, daughter of Alexander). In my head I called them Masha and Dasha. The mother, who seemed to me to be aged around 70 but was probably 30 or 40 years younger than that, had a shock of white bobbed hair. The daughter, around 14, had a shock of matching black bobbed hair. They were extremely careful, polite and softly spoken. They wore matching grey outdoor coats and highly polished shoes. They spoke very little and each sought permission to speak from the other with their eyes before saying anything. They looked like something out of *The Omen*. They were completely terrified of me, and I of them. This was the only thing we had in common.

They were even more terrified when they found out that I could already speak some Russian, and immediately observed tartly that some of the Russian I spoke was *mat* (profanity). Essentially there were two kinds of Russian: the Russian you spoke around people when you wanted them to think you were cultured and polite, and the Russian that everyone spoke with each other, especially younger people. I suppose the only equivalent we have in English is something like 'telephone voice' or 'talking posh' versus using slang. I knew a little about this distinction, but not enough to navigate it with any common sense. I just copied what other people said. I used words that lots of young people used every day like *tusovka* (a party or group of people) and *chuvak* (dude). I didn't mean to offend anyone; these were just the words I knew from listening to other Russians my age. When I explained to Masha and Dasha I was using words that my Russian friends used, the mother said that my friends must have been in prison. It was a bad start.

Looking back, I understand the culture clash a bit better and I feel ashamed: this poor woman and her daughter were conservative, cautious and sheltered. They hoped for a companion who would join them in needlecraft sessions and who could recite from *Valter Skott* – Soviet culture was obsessed with the 19th-century historical novelist Walter Scott, and people asked me endless questions about him with the same frequency that they asked me about the hunter and the fox in Ace of Base. Instead, someone had arrived in their quiet and well-ordered home who had lived at university for two years with no adult supervision, who was very grumpy about teaching English all day every day, and who had an immense craving for nicotine and a yearning to party. A far as my hosts were concerned, they were expecting Jane Austen, and they got Sid Vicious.

I lasted four days in their apartment. To be fair on Masha and Dasha, the timing of our encounter augured badly. It wasn't their fault that I moved in with them just as civil war nearly broke out. The three of us first heard about the political coup in Moscow from Dima, who came round to check up on me. It took him five minutes to walk round from his family's apartment. At this stage, the two of us were on good terms and I appreciated his concern. At least if Masha and Dasha murdered me in my sleep, someone would notice my absence. Dima had so far made a very poor impression on Masha and Dasha, probably by calling them 'dudes'. It was a Saturday, and he was often at a loose end on a Saturday evening as the parents of his girlfriend with the heart-shaped face didn't like her going out at night. Usually Dima expected to speak to me at the door of the apartment and not be allowed in. But on this occasion Masha and Dasha invited him in and listened to him intently. Something very bad must have happened.

I could half understand the expression *chrezvychainoe polozheniye*, a ridiculously difficult thing to pronounce, and they all kept saying it over and over. Masha and Dasha had a television that they never watched. They hurried to switch on the news, and the four of us sat awkwardly in a row on the edge of their sofa. A newsreader was saying a lot of things I didn't understand alongside more mentions of *chrezvychainoe polozheniye*. This sounded to me like *emergency position* and it didn't seem good. The correct translation is *state of emergency*. Masha gabbled something I had only read as a phrase in a book before: *Grazhdanskaya voina. Civil war.* Her face was white. The TV, however, was not saying *grazhdanskaya voina*. Was that a code? That if it didn't say it on the TV, then that probably meant it was actually happening? Or was it the other way around? That it couldn't be happening if they hadn't announced it on the TV? I looked out of the window. I couldn't see any civil war, just lots of lights on in apartments where you could see the exact same news report flickering on every TV screen.

I pieced together the information. It was an old-fashioned coup attempt, similar to the Black August one against Gorbachev in 1991. Yeltsin had been the hero of that failed putsch, rallying the liberals to face down the hardliners. In some ways Yeltsin had been too successful, although it was to his own benefit: Gorbachev was finished, and the Soviet Union collapsed. Now Yeltsin was

President and was continuing what Gorbachev had set in motion but not quite had the guts to pursue further: independence, democracy and free market capitalism. Nonetheless, the Communists were still not giving up easily.

The events of that autumn of 1993 were a clash between Boris Yeltsin and the Supreme Soviet. The old guard was back again, this time attempting to impeach Yeltsin. They had barricaded themselves in the White House in Moscow, hoping to gain momentum and support from people who wanted the Soviet Union back. It didn't work. Over the next ten days, there would be a stand-off which ended with the storming of the Ostankino TV centre by protesters loyal to Yeltsin. Russia was described as being 'on the brink of civil war', and a state of emergency was declared. Later, on TV, they showed shots being fired at civilians from inside the White House. During this period, 147 people died, including some foreign journalists.

But at that moment, we had no idea this was how things would turn out. All I wanted to know was: what does all this mean? Is it dangerous to be here? Over the next few hours, all the Brits who were staying with host families received phone calls from the organisers at the Vatson School of English to reassure us that they were keeping an eye on the situation. Dima and I went to a kids' playground, sat on the rusty swings, and smoked cigarettes until our fingers froze. I tried to get some sense out of him about whether we should be worried. He said what he always said about politics: that only foreigners cared about people like Boris Yeltsin. He would say 'Boris Yeltsin' in a fake American accent to make his point: it wasn't a name he was ever going to lower himself to say normally in his own voice. He was above caring about this kind of stuff. It was *sovok*. He had enjoyed the drama of breaking the news to Masha and Dasha, but he was not remotely bothered, and thought it would all blow over pretty quickly.

Masha and Dasha, on the other hand, were livid that we had gone out, and tried to forbid me from leaving the building. They had taken the news report much more seriously than Dima, and said they would be staying at home for the foreseeable future. They would appreciate it if I would do the same thing. Their reaction was unusual but not entirely unreasonable: there was a curfew in Moscow from 11pm to 5am. But the curfew did not extend to St Petersburg, and neither, it seemed, did the 'civil war'.

I was torn. I could see how scared they were. Yet I was still due to go and teach my class at the Vatson School of English the next day. If things were really that bad, they would have closed the school. I felt bad for Masha and Dasha: I was causing them unnecessary worry at this horrible time. And heaven knows what they had been through in their lives. For a start, I didn't know them well enough to ask why there was no Mister Masha. In their eyes, I was a foreigner leaving the house during the 'emergency position' to go and hang out with convicted criminals who used the word 'dude'. That night, while the two of them slept on the sofa bed in the living room, I cried myself to sleep in the bedroom they had given up for me. This was an adventure – but not the one I had been looking for.

The next day in class, none of my students seemed bothered, and muttered variations on the expression *Moskva bolshaya dereva*. This was a favourite saying of St Petersburgers: *Moscow is a big village*. Or they might shrug, wave a hand dismissively and say, *Eto Moskva. It's just Moscow being Moscow*. These phrases all expressed the same idea: Moscow is a long way away; Moscow is a law unto itself; Moscow is not St Petersburg. They didn't say it with much conviction. But I was rapidly learning not to probe too deeply or to expect people to explain things to me. They had clearly long stopped trying to explain the fragile peace in their fledgling country to themselves. What hope did they have of explaining it to a foreigner who was tripping over the landmine of consonants in *chrezvychainoe polozheniye*?

That night after classes, I dropped in on Dima's family on the way home, still trying to work out whether there was a civil war going on without me knowing about it. I was tired and weepy after a long day at school and the freezing commute home on a bone-shaking tram. Katya made me coffee and sat me down. She had had an idea. I could move in with them. Her husband was not expected back on leave for months. They could make space. We would just have to get the Vatson School of English to agree because my visa was officially registered with them. We both reasoned that if they moved me out, the powers-that-be would probably move other foreigners in with Masha and Dasha who might be happier there. Perhaps a mild-mannered accountant with an interest in chess, or someone studying the Kirov ballet. This would suit them very well.

I thought this was the perfect solution. The Vatson School of English would have to sort the finances: I had some extra money that I would pay to my 'new' family for now as I didn't want the 'old' family to be out of pocket. It wasn't their fault that it hadn't worked out. Katya made the phone call to the English school the next day. Arrangements were made. I moved out immediately. Masha and Dasha took it very badly and chose to blame the situation on my terrible personality, which was probably not grossly inaccurate. But they were also clearly relieved – and they were probably going to get double the money for a while if another foreigner could be allocated to them.

By Tuesday, Yeltsin was back in control, and I had moved out. And yet, I did not feel as relieved as I had expected. After all, I had got what I wanted, hadn't I? Katya was doing me a real favour: I was grateful to her. But I couldn't help but feel that in escaping one unsuitable situation, I had simply landed myself in another.

*   *   *

By this point, I was a few weeks into my new life of getting up at the crack of dawn to front up to a class of blank-faced Russian adult learners who hated me. Month One had been Acclimatisation. Months Two to Ten would be Classroom Teaching: English Immersion. Except I did not feel especially acclimatised, my students were barely immersed and my classroom teaching was a disaster.

Every morning, I would head out into the freezing cold to the tram stop on Vasilievsky Island en route to the Vatson School of English. I would be shivering and grumpy, but I didn't mind waiting outside in the cold, because travelling on the metro alone scared me. You got jostled and poked and prodded, and you never got a seat. On the tram, I could get a seat by the window and see the best view in the world: the sun rising over the green and white icing façade of the cake-like Winter Palace, the first light of the morning reflected off St Isaac's Cathedral. I told myself that this view was why I had left home for a year, why I was tolerating living in extremely small spaces with people I didn't really know, why I was up so early going to a job I didn't really want.

Although I grumbled, I secretly loved that commute. The tracks groaned as the tram rounded a corner; we snaked around a side street and headed into the atmospheric part of the city Dostoevsky describes in *Crime and Punishment*, the quarter around Sennaya Ploschad, the old hay market, where the tram passes alongside Kanal Griboyedova. The open view across the river to the Hermitage is spectacular, but I loved this hidden, atmospheric corner of the city in the morning light, with all its imposing façades and the glassy canal.

Some of the lessons were early so that the adult students, all Russians aged between their early twenties and late sixties, could get to work afterwards. Other lessons were at the end of their working day. I taught both. My classes were both terrifying and amusing. When I first arrived at the start of that academic year, I had under-gone half-hearted training in the teaching of English. We were told that we were not allowed to use any Russian in class. If our students were exposed only to our native language, they would allegedly learn quickly and easily.

By the end of my students' first day of English Immersion, a sea of irritated and bewildered faces convinced me otherwise. Two grown women started to cry. After four days my class still did not speak any English. Or at least, they were not comfortable speaking it out loud, in front of me. English was compulsory at school, and I had no doubt that they knew some. But once they noticed the yawning gap between what they had learned and the way I spoke, they clammed up.

It was obvious that I was going to have to start speaking Russian to them. Unfortunately, I did not really speak enough Russian to teach them properly, a fact which became apparent pretty fast. A couple of the men went to the course organisers and complained: the British students were too young to teach, they didn't know any Russian, it was a waste of money. They were told to be patient.

This was at a time when many people had never even heard a foreigner speaking Russian. We were a novelty, a freak show. So this approach worked for a bit. The trouble is you can probably only get people to pay to see a freak show once. Our interactions became tiring for both parties. The class laughed at me the first time that I inadvertently announced I would be urinating on the blackboard. Get the stress wrong on the word *pisat'* (to write, when the emphasis is on the second syllable), and you are saying the word *pisat'* (to piss, with the emphasis on the first syllable). Welcome to the Russian language. The second time it happened they were cross with me. *Udareniye*, they muttered. *Get the stress on the right syllable. It's not difficult.*

My fellow British student teachers were also struggling. None of us could get our classes much further than 'What is your name?' We comforted ourselves with two reported breakthroughs. The convention in Russia is to identify yourself according to your name and patronymic: Ivan Ivanovich – Ivan, son of Ivan. We had decided to ban full names because they were too Russian. But in my friend's class, two of her students had been angsting about how to identify themselves using first names only. Both these students were called Dryusha (short for Andrei). One always wore a green polo neck, and after much confusion, he suddenly exclaimed in English, 'He is Dryusha. I am Dryusha Green.'

The second breakthrough took place in my class. A beautiful young woman, probably the closest person to me in age out of all of them, put her hand up and proclaimed dramatically, 'My name is Snezhana and I am an art.' Snezhana means – gloriously – *She of the Snow*. And she was an artist. It was a noble attempt at breaking the communication deadlock. Perhaps we were getting somewhere after all.

It wasn't until I met Bogdan that things really took off, though. The day after we first met, I had arrived at work still wearing the same clothes as the day before. This had not gone unnoticed, and questions were clearly asked behind my back. Word of God's Gift travelled fast. People in my class had friends in other classes who were taught by British students, some of whom had been at Kosmos when I first met him. Between them, they pieced together information. Dryusha Green got his dictionary out. 'Teacher knows a gentleman from Ukraine?' Who needs the KGB? 'Can you rephrase that as a "Do you . . .?" question?' I replied.

You have to turn these situations to your advantage. A potential love affair finally gave my students the impetus to ask me questions, and I could force them to ask the questions in English. It was completely unprofessional and not what we had been taught on the training course, but letting them ask whatever they wanted about my private life was an effective teaching strategy, so I stuck to it.

We got used to each other's ways, but I never quite got used to the spectacle of the class. In the early days, I had to stop myself doing a doubletake. Several of the men had 1970s handlebar moustaches, and a number of the women wore astonishing green or blue eyeshadow and/or bright pink frosted lipstick. The clothes reminded me of TV shows from home that were already so old that they were shown on repeat: *Starsky and Hutch*, *Minder*, *The Sweeney*. When I had first arrived the year before, I had been mesmerised by the look of people on the street. On the bus from the airport, I could barely believe what I was seeing. People walked down the street looking as if they were in a documentary from decades past, wearing beige flared three-piece suits, bell-bottomed jeans and safari jackets with huge lapels. That summer, Dima turned up for a date once wearing white tasselled leather moccasins and a matching white leather jacket. The jacket was slightly too small for him and, from the way he walked, it seemed the shoes were too. Clearly, he had borrowed these items from a smaller person. Possibly this was the head-to-toe 'get lucky' look used by an entire cohort? He wore it with the swagger of John Travolta in *Saturday Night Fever*, albeit with a mild limp.

It wasn't just the clothing that was outdated by Western standards. Before I started teaching, I had been vaguely aware of the work of Charles Ewart Eckersley, the author of the English textbook every Russian seemed to have at home. Dima's sister had already shown me his books. The Russians reverentially called him 'Ickersli' and so I too adopted this pronunciation. 'Ickersli' was the name on the only English textbook I ever came across in Russia, and as such he was regarded as the seminal authority on the correct use of English. I found out much later that Ickersli himself was a teacher in the 1920s and 1930s at schools that specialised in teaching English as a foreign language, a fairly new idea at that time.

Sometimes in class, people would say an incomprehensible phrase in English and others around them would nod sagely and intone, 'Ickersli'. It was a sort of bible, basically. But its prevalence also explained why so many people I met had studied English but not actually learned to speak it. The book had no conversational phrases in it, and contained almost nothing anyone would actually say in real life. It was just grammar without context. The design and feel reminded me of the 'Peter and Jane' books I had learned to read with at primary school in the 1970s. Ickersli was babyish, and yet at the same time so weird and antiquated that it was barely suitable for children or adults. One page vividly depicted cute bob-tailed bunnies bouncing around in a field next to a drawing of rabbits strung up in a butcher's shop, ready to be skinned. The English you were supposed to learn to go alongside this? 'These rabbits are alive. Those rabbits are dead.'

Was it really necessary to teach from this book? Surely there must be hundreds of other options? The trouble was, in the Soviet world, it was the only thing available. Ickersli had not been updated in decades simply because there was no reason to update it. English was taught in schools as a discipline and as a way of showing off. It was an academic exercise and a point of pride. As long as you taught English in schools, how could you be accused of being cut off from the world? It was also seen as an important part of being cultured: if you knew about English literature and customs, no one could accuse you of being stupid and ignorant.

Sometimes, though, I wondered if the state apparatus had made a deliberate choice to teach only basic English so that all things Russian would appear so much more advanced as a result. Forget 'essential' English (and English could not have been less of an essential in Soviet life) – the truth was that in the USSR you were absolutely not supposed to progress beyond Ickersli and actually travel anywhere, or speak to anyone, anyway. Any conversation about small mammals, whether living or recently deceased, was never going to happen.

In that sense, our encounters were radical: these were adults born in the 1950s and 1960s who had perhaps never expected to meet a foreigner in their lifetimes. They had learned English in the same

way I learned Latin at school: not in the hope of conversing with a
Roman centurion, but as an academic exercise. Now, whenever we
understood each other or made each other laugh, it contradicted a
view of reality they had held for years. Being an adult learner in a
classroom with a blackboard is a humbling experience. And in a way
it was a stroke of genius to have these classes taught by Brits barely
out of their teens: we were young and stupid, and our Russian was
embarrassing. It levelled the playing field.

For me, the students were an information resource. I could ask
them where to buy stuff like a winter coat. I could check if I was
using the correct verb form in a sentence. I could ask them about
food I didn't understand like *sushki*, the weird, flavourless rusk
biscuits that Dima soaked in his tea. Did everyone eat these? They
were horrified I didn't like *sushki*. They taught me more Russian
than I taught them English.

I could also ask them about words that I didn't want to check
with Dima, Katya or Inessa. The morning after I met Bogdan, as I
stumbled into class, I had an urgent, burning need to find out what
chuchelo meant. *Ty prosto chuchelo. You're simply* . . . Simply what? I
had already looked in a dictionary and couldn't find it. Had I heard
the word wrong? I knew if I asked anyone I knew they would want
to know the context. I asked Snezhana, my favourite student. She
began to draw a strange shape on the blackboard. At first it looked
like a messy scribble. Slowly, an image of a scarecrow standing in
a field emerged, its arms outstretched and a scraggy crow perched
nearby. She pointed at the picture. *Chuchelo.* Yep, it was a scarecrow.
She smiled. *V printsipye, kak by idiyot. It's also a slang word for idiot.*

* * *

Having avoided civil war, moved in with Dima's family and fallen in love with God's Gift all in the same week, I tried to settle down. After that first night in the hostel, Bogdan and I spent the weekend together, inseparable. Or rather, I was inseparable from him, as I followed 'Ukraine answer to Red Hot Chili Pepper' around from nightclub to cigarette kiosk and back again. After they left, I spent more time at home than usual, waiting for him to call and let me know when he was next in town. He was supposed to be back within the month.

Inessa and Katya would catch me looking off into the distance. 'He has such a beautiful name. Bogdan Bogdanovich. Gift of God, son of Gift of God.' Inessa sighed. As we waited for him to phone, Inessa wanted to be the one to answer. At 11, these things seemed dreamy, romantic and exciting to her. She loved to talk about party dresses and hairstyles and all the new adverts for things on television that were shiny and desirable. I was expected to explain these things and translate them, both in terms of what the words meant – 'Yes, Uncle Ben is *Dyadya* Ben just like *Dyadya* Vanya is Uncle Vanya' – and in terms of what they were as physical items. I gave up trying to find the words for 'boil-in-the-bag' and said we should just buy some Uncle Ben's. *Dorogo, zhe! I prosto ris.* Katya would tut. *So expensive. I mean, it's just rice.*

I could have bought these things for them with my carefully counted money, but I didn't. First, because I didn't want to take the risk that they would end up liking these things more than what they already had. Second, because I didn't want anyone to think that I thought these things were better. Because I didn't anyway. That year David Remnick, Moscow correspondent for *The Washington Post*, published a book called *Lenin's Tomb: The Last Days of the Soviet*

Empire. In it, he wrote about a real-life museum called the Exhibition of Poor Quality Goods, a self-flagellating, depressing display of items – from broken alarm clocks to piles of rotting cabbage – supposed to memorialise or exorcise the ghost of Soviet incompetence. I never visited the Exhibition of Poor Quality Goods, but I always felt that Russians were subconsciously inviting me to submit entries for it. Constantly I heard people say things like, 'Of course, I'm sure this is not as good as what you have in the West . . .', and I would constantly have to reply, 'No, no, this is delicious, this is wonderful, this is better than what we have.'

People were anxious and sad and humiliated all at once, but also over-excited about Uncle Ben's and Bounty. They either dug deep into self-denigration, or made preposterous assertions about home-grown phenomena. *Eskimo* ice cream must be unlike anything I had ever tasted before. I couldn't possibly have experienced real opera or ballet until I had seen Russian opera and ballet. Western soup was vastly inferior to *borsch* and *shchi* (cabbage soup). There was no middle ground between these extremes of inferiority and superiority, and people see-sawed up and down between them in the same conversation.

I would fall into the same hyperbole myself, wanting to conform and flatter and make myself sound as if I belonged; that I would never, ever compare anything negatively to whatever we had back home. *Bezuslovno, certainly not*! And then in the next breath, I'd mutter *sovok* if a kiosk attendant slammed the window shut for a 'technical break' just as I stepped forward to ask for Marlboro Menthols (yes, it had come to this). There was a sort of complicity to surviving in this environment and you simply had to give in to it. The writer and Nobel Prize winner Svetlana Alexievich once described herself as an 'accomplice' to the Soviet experience: how she herself was a true believer, a 'Little Octobrist' and a Pioneer – rites of passage of a typical Soviet childhood, like the Brownies or the Scouts ('Disillusionment came later,' she wrote). She describes those born in the USSR and those born after as being 'from different planets'. But what if you're not in either of those categories? What if you're from another galaxy? I wasn't born into the system or after the system, but I still had to find a way to fit in.

* * *

Inessa's excitement at the prospect of *roman* (a romance) – was catching and I allowed myself to be as childishly thrilled as she was. This was a time when we were all almost as innocent as Inessa in some ways. There were no shortcuts to knowledge or experience when all of life was lived offline. Before the internet, before WhatsApp, before Google Maps, we were all at the same disadvantage, whether Soviet or Western. There were only two ways of finding out anything: either you looked it up in a book, or you asked another human being. This was true of both factual information and more subjective life experience. The rest of the time, you lived in your imagination or, if you were lucky, you might pick up some scrap from TV or radio – but even then, you had to chance upon it by accident, and couldn't re-access it on demand. Even though Inessa was 11 and I was 20, we both wanted to figure out a lot of things that we could only learn by living through it or by asking other people what it was like. The only way to find answers was to get to know people, to talk to them, to make the effort to be patient. This created a trust, a

63

curiosity and a healthy interdependence that I sometimes think has disappeared without trace.

There was a downside to this innocence and openness. It made you vulnerable, and it made you dependent. During the time I spent in the former Soviet Union in the early 1990s, I put myself in situations that were at best unpredictable and at worst predictably dangerous. I picked up hangers-on and random people, and spent hours talking to them and getting drunk with them. I cultivated intense friendships – blood brothers stuff – with people with whom I could not really communicate. I attached myself blindly to an excessively good-looking man at a single glance. I look back now and think: go home and have an early night. Do not stay overnight in the Pistachio Prison. Do not try and absorb fluent Russian by speaking to every single person you meet and hanging on their every word. Calm down. But more than that I think: do not go and live with Dima's family. Because all the goodness and sweetness of Inessa and Katya could not offset the fact that the situation with Dima was a bomb waiting to go off.

After I met Bogdan, I became very popular with everyone else, including my once-wary students, and very unpopular with Dima. Katya and Inessa were incredibly indulgent of me, and would never have dreamed of asking me where I had been or what I was doing, unless to tease me or be a bit nosy. They waited for me to talk. 'Tell me again about his eyes,' Inessa would sigh, her hand cupping her chin. 'Inessa, leave Vipulya alone,' her mother would chide. Then she would cup her chin in her hand herself and sigh, 'I wonder when he's coming back?' They respected the fact that I had British friends and other Russian friends and the Dryusha Greens of this world to think about. I don't think Dima's mum would have treated a Russian daughter of the same age in the same way. But she saw that I was not Russian and not her daughter, and so she let me be. She took what I told her on my terms: if I was excited to meet someone, she was excited for me.

With Dima, it was another matter. He was still livid that I had been going to Kosmos without him. And he was livid about me meeting these 'random Ukrainians'. Now he didn't want me seeing British friends unless I took him with me. They might introduce me to Russians that he didn't know. They could be from Moscow, or anywhere. He wanted to vet anyone coming into my orbit. He was trying to go everywhere with me, something that had long been a bone of contention between us. I did not need a chaperone. *Pochemu nelzya odna? Why can't I go on my own?* He simply scowled. *Nelzya. It is not allowed.* I didn't know how to say, 'Who died and made you king?' in Russian, but I would give him a look that said this, and congratulate myself inwardly on finding an alternative translation: *Ty ne moi otets'* This I did know how to say. *You are not my father.*

He could say *nelzya* as much as he wanted – I would still go. I was learning, in any case, that *nelzya* had many meanings. In theory, it meant *it is not allowed* or *it is forbidden*. If it was used in an official context, you had to obey it. Formally, it was an absolute restriction. But in an unofficial context – or a personal one – it often meant *I know better than you*. And that, as we all know, is not the same as something actually being forbidden.

I still think about the word *nelzya* a lot. It has a fluid and flexible meaning in Russian, and there is no real equivalent in English. It's a brilliant illustration of control. Is it really forbidden to do this thing?

In what sense 'forbidden'? Is it illegal? Ill-advised? Morally wrong? Or is it just forbidden in the sense that someone wants you to do as you're told? *Nelzya* glosses over all these distinctions and says: don't think about why, just don't do it. To me, *nelzya* was a problematic word. But now it was Dima's favourite word.

winter, n.
зима, zima (Russian)
зима, zyma (Ukrainian)

After the night I met Bogdan, the Ukrainians disappeared off to Moscow, promising to return the following month. To my lovesick amazement, they came back as they said they would, for four or five nights. This was going to be a regular thing; they had some kind of vague monthly residency. They had gigs at Kosmos and at other places around town, and I would turn up to these and hang out with Bogdan. At their gigs, the Colney Hatch guys mostly soundchecked, and I sat around drinking Baltika beer and smoking cigarettes with all the other hangers-on connected to the club or to other bands. Some of the guys who came and went were 'sponsors.' They bankrolled the band on and off, occasionally handing out a hundred dollars or so 'for expenses'. When I met these 'businessmen', who styled themselves as the band's 'managers', it was always hard for me to work out whether these people were genuine entrepreneurs, fantasists or hardened criminals. It was never clear how exactly they made their money; they would mumble things like 'import-export'.

Often the 'managers' were old friends from school days who were passing through St Petersburg. They underwrote the band because they wanted to be cool by association, because they felt guilty having money when their friends didn't have any, and because – although this really was a stretch – they wanted credit and profit if 'Ukraine answer to Red Hot Chili Pepper' ever hit the big time.

There was an older man, a Russian named Kuznetsov, who hung around with all the bands, always wearing a brightly coloured 1980s ski jacket. Everyone called him by his surname, which was a way of dismissing him. If you knew and liked someone, you called them by their first name and patronymic. Kuznetsov fancied himself as the 'manager of managers', and was forever trying to muscle in on conversations and talk to Artem, the singer, about Colney Hatch's future. No one liked him, and I felt a bit sorry for him, which meant he would often come and sit next to me.

He once asked me out for coffee, unexpectedly, saying he had something very important to ask me that would affect Bogdan's future. We met at Baskin-Robbins, which had just opened. As the months passed, more foreign goods were appearing, and more expensive new shops were opening. Meanwhile, the same old post-Soviet stores still had the same old queues. 'Here – *zdes* – you can eat as much ice cream as you like,' Kuznetsov said, smiling, his gold tooth winking at me. He explained that he was a businessman and had a serious proposition: I had to break Colney Hatch in the West. I was the only person who could do it.

I nearly spat out a mouthful of over-priced ice cream. He explained to me that there was this thing called 'A&R', which was the part of record companies that scouted for talent. You could send them tapes and they would listen to the tapes and then sign you up for a record deal. He said that he couldn't contact them from Russia, 'but you can contact them. When you go home.' I tried not to roll my eyes. He countered, 'Everyone knows how you feel about Bogdan. This is the only way he has a chance. If you do something.'

It was emotional blackmail via novelty ice cream. And it worked. I said I would do what I could when I got back to England. There was an innocent part of me that understood what he was saying and agreed with him: the chances of the band ever coming to anything without someone in the West picking up on them were minimal, so I may as well do whatever I could. In the back of my mind, I knew exactly how far-fetched this 'business plan' was. But everyone needs a dream in this life. And now it was up to me. I was a clueless, lovesick, pedantic linguist. But I held the future of Ukrainian rock 'n' roll in my hands.

* * *

By the third time the Ukrainians came back, the temperature was regularly -5C in the mornings when I travelled to work. Sometimes it was as low as -10C. It was tough on the spirit unless you were someone who wanted to stay indoors all the time. And I was not that kind of someone. Daydreaming about Bogdan was the thing that kept my morale up. I would tell myself that I was young, I was in love and I was living in an amazing city, even if the hairs inside my nose did freeze into miniature icicles daily on the commute to work.

When the band rolled into town the second time, I had thought it was a fluke, and wondered if I might never see them again. But now I had started to trust what Bogdan said: they really did have a monthly residency, they really would be here every month, and we really would get to spend the summer together. It didn't occur to either of us that we had any other options. It wasn't as if I could just throw in my teaching course and go to Ukraine. And it wasn't as if he could give up the band and come and live with me in Russia. Of course, I wondered if Bogdan had other girlfriends or a whole other life. But he was so laid-back that somehow this seemed incredibly unlikely. Daydreaming maintained a lot of relationships in those days, when you couldn't look anyone up online and get a reality check.

He never called when he was away, which was disappointing for Inessa, but otherwise not that big a deal. This was a place not everyone had a telephone at home. The *sovkovy* postal service was wildly unreliable and incredibly slow. If you were really desperate you could send a telegram. There was no expectation that contact was easy or necessary, and so you just waited to see people when you saw them.

Even if you could get to a telephone, the owners wouldn't be that happy for you to use it for long-distance calls because they were so expensive. Given the rate of inflation, it was never clear how much the bill would come to when it arrived, so I rarely made international calls home to my family and didn't write to them either. At first, I called my parents maybe once a month. Then came a point later in the year when I just didn't call them at all. Undeterred, my sister, three years younger than me, continued to send me long letters recounting the plots of *Neighbours* and *Home and Away*, which arrived months after she had written them, often out of sequence. The way I cut myself off from home wasn't typical, but it also wasn't that unusual: it was quite difficult *not* to disappear if you went some-where like Russia.

Locally, though, phone calls were free within the city limits. It was common to use the phone – a landline, naturally – to continue a conversation that you had just been having in person. *Pozvoni kak srazu priidyosh. Call me as soon as you get in.* People used the phone not to keep in touch with distant friends and family, but to have non-stop chats with their local mates – for hours. Because these phone calls were free, adults used the telephone like kids used to play with walkie-talkies. They had telephones with very long cords that stretched across a whole apartment. Sometimes, you would hold up the receiver and talk no matter what you were doing: cooking dinner, reading a book, watching TV. It felt as if you could pick up the phone and somebody would already be on the other end, waiting to talk.

And so it was that Misha, a Ukrainian friend of Bogdan's who lived in St Petersburg, started to call me on a regular basis. We would talk for hours. I had met Misha a couple of days after meeting the other guys in the band. He turned up at Kosmos to drop off a bag of stuff for them to take home to his family. He was from the same hometown, and had relocated to St Petersburg to finish his university studies and get some kind of long-term work.

Although he was an old schoolmate of the band's, Misha seemed like an incredibly unlikely part of their retinue. The band all hung out in nightclubs and dressed like Bon Jovi roadies. Misha hated Kosmos and dressed like an accountant. The band had long hair, cultivated a permanent five o'clock shadow, and thought a denim jacket was enough of an outdoor coat when the snow was lying thick on the ground. Misha had a selection of sensible full-length gentlemen's coats, was scrupulously clean-shaven and always wore a trilby. His hair was cut into the sort of neat hairstyle that looked as if he was on his way to a job interview. This turned out later to be appropriate: officially he was finishing his PhD, but in reality he was constantly on the lookout for work. One of the many part-time temporary jobs he managed to secure in the year that I knew him was to be what he called – in English, with a flourish – 'agent of estate'.

Misha was an organised and grown-up person with his own apartment, which was where the band usually stayed when they were in St Petersburg. He was also the only one of the Ukrainians who had a telephone. Bogdan had initially taken 'my' phone number when we first met – or, rather, the phone number of Dima's apartment, which was a problem – but I had no way of contacting him. There wasn't a telephone in the places where he hung out in Moscow and his parents back home in Ukraine didn't have one either: if they wanted to call anyone, they had to go to a neighbour's or use a payphone. This is how Misha ended up taking my number and becoming our go-between. When one of the guys in the band called Misha from the road to tell them their plans, he would call me and let me know what was going on.

Not only did Bogdan not have access to a telephone, he didn't like using one much either. Misha's telephone manner, by contrast, was a joy to behold. Inessa and Katya would fight to answer the phone in the hope it was him. Both mother and daughter swooned as they relayed his messages and imitated his opening gambits with great reverence and admiration. These linguistic stylings went something like: '*Allo* [the universal phone greeting]? Good evening to you, dear respected lady. I beg your forgiveness for this disturbance.

Please, would you possibly be so kind, indeed would you conceivably consider being the soul of goodness in this manner? Could you possibly entertain passing the telephone receiver to Vivka, if it is not too much trouble?' This was very different to most people's phone greeting which was usually, *A Vivku mozhno? – is Vivka there? –* without a hello or niceties of any kind.

Misha had the gift of the gab. On or off the telephone, he possessed the ability to talk in the 'phone voice' cultured Soviet way that impressed people like Masha and Dasha. This was linked to the Soviet ideal of knowledge, self-improvement and education. It was also about excellence in the Russian language. Russian, like Latin, has many cases depending on where a word sits in a sentence. It's common for Russians to swallow the endings of words to disguise the fact that they're not too sure of a case ending. It is immensely satisfying as a foreigner when you realise this is happening, and that *even Russians* think Russian is a nightmare. Except Misha, a Ukrainian who spoke both native Russian and native Ukrainian. His case endings were always flawless and rang out clear as a bell.

You would never say to a native English speaker, 'Oh, you speak beautiful English!' Instead, you might say that someone is articulate. But it was common for Russians to compliment each other on their native Russian, if it was particularly accurate, clear or impressively flowery. In a Western sense, this might not seem an anti-establishment way to talk, quite the opposite in fact. But for Russian speakers like Misha, speaking beautifully was a way of rising above the mess around them, of demonstrating self-respect and of standing out – all without offending anyone or attacking the status quo.

Misha excelled at this. And not only was his Russian beautiful, so was his Ukrainian. He was the first person to explain to me the differences between the two languages and, years later, he was the first person who ever talked to me about Ukrainian independence, Ukrainian nationalism and the importance of speaking Ukrainian instead of Russian. He would encourage me to master difficult phrases. On the metro I was fascinated by the collision of consonants in the announcement: *Ostorozhno, dveri zakryyayutsya. Attention, doors are closing.* Once I'd got it, we moved onto the Ukrainian equivalent: *Oberezhno, dveri zachinyayuts'ya.* Misha said it sounded so much more beautiful in Ukrainian. I shrugged and rolled my eyes. They were both a mouthful. And who would ever need to know both?

*   *   *

Bogdan, for all his sweetness and God-given gifts, was not much of a talker. He was shy and silent. He couldn't hold a room, or organise anything, or make things happen. Misha, meanwhile, could talk for hours; soon we had established endless jokes and sayings and catchphrases, and we made each other laugh. Misha became like a brother and a protector to me.

Even though it was obvious to everyone over the course of that year that out of the entire group, Misha and I were basically soulmates, there was no hint of romance between us. We were just never physically attracted to each other. Or at least: I didn't fancy him, and if he had feelings for me, he was religiously discreet about it. Any kind of look that might have suggested anything else never passed between us. Which was a relief, because it would have made me avoid him completely. I didn't need more complications.

I soon felt comfortable with the Ukrainians. In many ways, all these young men, with their own messy lives and hopes and dreams and Soviet hang-ups, looked after me as if we were family. Borys and Artem were friendly and made it obvious they wanted Bogdan to have a girlfriend. They had their own 'wives' back at home. The word 'wife' was – like so many concepts at this time – nebulous. It didn't necessarily mean you were married, and it was rude to ask for legal details, but it did usually mean that you had a girlfriend you were serious about. I liked it when they talked about their 'wives'. It kept things safe and normal.

Of all the guys in the band, it was Borys for whom I had the softest spot, in a purely sisterly way. He was shorter than me, with a wiry, Iggy Pop, pipe-cleaner kind of body. He looked as if he could have been an escapologist in another life. He had a ferretlike sort of face, a sharp nose with huge nostrils and long, straggly, wild blonde hair. He was magnificent. And disturbing. I was a fan of his because he was the messiest and most unpredictable of the gang. The others seemed almost as if they were playing at being pop stars because this was a point in time when it seemed like a good moment to give it a go. Borys was rock 'n' roll at any point in space and time. I could imagine the other guys having office jobs or doing some other creative thing. I could even imagine Artem, the lead singer, cutting his hair short and becoming the manager of a branch of McDonald's. But with Borys, I could not imagine him doing anything other than this. He was the real deal.

He was also attractive as a person because he was extremely comfortable in his wiry little body. He never paid for the metro and always snuck through the gates behind someone else, like a small Dickensian urchin. He wore trousers that barely fit him – almost like a child's jeans, they were so tiny. And he would strip off at every opportunity: because it was hot, because his T-shirt was getting in the way of his bass guitar, because he felt like it. It wasn't to show off his body or make anyone feel uncomfortable, it was just because he felt more at ease that way. Once, we went on a boat trip on the river and I laughed so hard at something that my sunglasses fell off the back of my head and into the Neva. I wasn't remotely worried as the glasses were cheap and easily replaced, so I just laughed more at how clumsy I was. In a split second, though, Borys had stripped his clothes off down to a pair of baggy white-grey Y-fronts and taken a dive off the side of the boat, emerging triumphant with the sunglasses between his teeth.

*   *   *

The better I got to know the Ukrainians, the more I fell in love with Bogdan, the more I relied on Misha. And, crucially, the more tense things got with Dima. He had favours to ask. He needed my help. He wanted me to come on this or that errand with him.

Dima had a friend who wanted a visa. Could I contact the UK authorities and sort out an invitation? I'd done it for him when he came to England, so why would it be difficult a second time, even if it was someone I didn't know? I managed to say no by mumbling a lot and making excuses. These tests were about my loyalty. Was I grateful enough to him and his family for rescuing me? Was I *nash* (ours) enough? Or was I one of *them*? Could I be relied on to choose him over some *khokhol*?

Dima loved to talk about *khokhly*, the slang word for Ukrainians. He used the word *khokhol* (*khokhly* is the plural) to describe them, which is like the French saying *les rosbifs* for the English and us saying *those frogs* for the French, only much more offensive. *Khokhol* is the Russian word for *Cossack topknot*, meaning a tuft of hair protruding like a mohawk from a shaven head. Depending on who you are, it's a colloquial, humorous expression (if you are a Russian nationalist) or an ethnic slur (if you are Ukrainian). I heard Ukrainians use it ironically in reference to themselves, messing about. I never heard a Russian use it in front of Ukrainians. Dima used it all the time, which was one of the many reasons that I had never introduced him to any of the Ukrainians, and had no intention of doing so. This annoyed him profoundly. How could he know if it was safe for me to hang out with people if he hadn't personally vetted them?

One minute he was so angry with me that he couldn't look at me, and the next he wanted to accompany me everywhere – but only when it was convenient to him. He was a bully, but at least he was an inconsistent one. I grew closer to Katya and Inessa, and tried to ignore the feeling that Dima was watching my every move. He understood that he was not my boyfriend, since I regularly had to remind him. But he had *once* been my boyfriend, and he wasn't going to forget about it entirely. He wanted to know where I went, when I was coming home, and who I was hanging out with. And soon he would start saying things like, *Zachem tebye eti khokhly? What do you need those Ukrainians for?*

* * *

I was sick of trying to appease everyone, of trying to be simultaneously ingratiating and wary, of trying to work out what people were saying to me and whether it was something important or something completely mad. There was a battle between two ideas in my head: how to be safe and how to be independent. In my normal university life back home, I was both things effortlessly and barely had to think about it. Here, I constantly felt as if I was missing something. There were things people weren't telling me: like whether I should stick to changing dollars at the official kiosk as I liked to, or whether I should give in to the student in my class who was pestering me to change them with him for a better rate. Or whether it really was dangerous for me to walk home from work on my own at night, as Dima insisted it was. Or whether there definitely was or wasn't a civil war.

I decided the answer was to improve my Russian to the point where I would become less dependent and could figure things out entirely for myself. After class with my students, and with friends like Misha, I was starting to broach difficult subjects. As my Russian improved, there were things I wanted to know. Even though sometimes I wasn't quite sure what it was exactly that I was trying to ask, let alone how to phrase it in Russian.

I felt there were unspoken currents beneath the surface. I wanted to know, for example, if the KGB still had any kind of hold over people's lives. When I had first visited the former Soviet Union in August 1992, there was still the idea amongst foreigners that someone from the KGB might follow you. By the time I had gone to live there on my own a year later, I knew this was nonsense, despite what everyone assumed from years of propaganda and spy films. I had arrived too late for the days of the KGB tail. But still I wanted to know: was there anything that I could do wrong that could get me into trouble? What about Russian friends? Could I get *them* into trouble without realising? Was anyone around us likely to be – or to have been – KGB?

The KGB's full name translates as 'Committee of State Security'. In 1991, the state it was supposed to safeguard had dissolved. Ostensibly it had failed in its most basic task, and so it, too, had dissolved. But in reality, everyone knew that a giant system like that doesn't disappear overnight. It morphed into other organisations under various acronyms, until in 1995 it became – and remains – the FSB, or Federal Security Service. And you could hardly call the FSB irrelevant: Putin became director of the FSB in 1998 and 1999. So why did no one talk about it?

Apart from the KGB, I wanted to know who was and who wasn't in the Communist Party, and whether that mattered. I had questions about *glasnost* and *perestroika* and Gorbachev and Yeltsin, and what people 'really thought'. I had been trying to ask about these things since my first visit, but my efforts then were clumsy and confrontational. Instead of opening up, people closed down and just told the joke I had heard so many times: 'An American and a Russian are arguing about free speech. The American says, "We have total freedom. I can go to the White House and shout, 'Go to hell, Bill Clinton.'" The Russian replies, "We also have total freedom. I too can go to Kremlin and shout, 'Go to hell, Bill Clinton.'"'

Most of all, I wanted to know how safe people felt, and what their political views were. I was genuinely curious. But I suppose I was also looking for reassurance, and perhaps for a sign that things were broadly OK and that it was safe for me to live independently as an adult in this place instead of like someone's overgrown adopted child.

I tried to find a better way to ask, and as I found the language and the courage to broach these subjects, I soon learned that this was what people of my age thought: they thought nothing. They said they didn't care about any of these things, and they thought it was funny that I thought they would care. In response to my questions I would get the words *pofig* or *po-barabanu*. The first means *don't care*. The second comes from an expression which means *I am so indifferent to your words that they bounce off me as if I were a drum*. (You can say what you like about Russian but it's not a dull language.) I had long discussions with Misha about the conclusions to be drawn from these responses. I don't believe that the people I knew refused to discuss these things with me while talking about them freely elsewhere. Of course, there were other people who were dissidents or who followed the news. But these people were not in the circles I was in. The people I knew had intentionally cut themselves off from politics completely. When I tried to talk to older people, I sensed they thought something, but not anything they wanted to get into with me. Either way, none of the conversations I had reassured me.

If I asked too much, or pushed into the territory of 'But you must have some opinion . . .', they would get angry and call me naive, bourgeois, Western, foreign, not *nash* (one of ours). They might say, *Eto ty tolko po-tvoemu – that's just you taking it your way*. It was *ne po-nashemu – not our way*. If someone was being kind or trying to explain their indifference, they might use the word *vospriyatiye*. It was all a question of *perception*. And we couldn't possibly have the same *perception*. They saw these ideas and topics as being things that people are interested in Over There, where I came from. Here they carried no meaning and were not topics for conversation . . .. *Nam vso ravno. It's all the same to us*. No one cares.

Nothing anyone told me reassured me. The conclusion I drew from all this was that the only way to feel safe here was to pass for local. Perhaps if I could just disappear into the crowd, vanish into everyday life, I would be OK. It was the only route to any kind of independence: if people thought you were just another citizen going about your business in the post-Soviet world, they didn't bother you. I became obsessional about this, and whenever I managed to be alone I would set little challenges for myself, trying to figure out if I could pass. Looking back, this was the start of me losing sight of the person I had been before that year, someone who was anchored and had reasonably good judgement. But it was also the start of me becoming more confident in Russian. And so I didn't care much about the cost.

The tram I took to work every morning would wheeze and creak around the Sennaya Ploschad, threatening to get stuck as the temperature dropped and the rails froze. When this happened, I would get out and walk. Or sometimes I would get out a few stops early just because I felt like it, and go round some of the stalls at the market.

These moments were a good test for me and my Russian. Could I understand what people called out to me? 'Girl, try this sour cream.' 'Little girl, look at these apples.' 'Little sunshine, come over here.' And if I could understand, what did I say back? How should I behave if I say nothing? Should I smile and walk on? Could I pass for local if I said nothing? And the biggest challenge: could I pass for local if I opened my mouth? The stallholders were raucous, the market was often crowded, and even the shortest of conversations with them could be exposing. They might challenge me by switching into English: 'Oy, *khallo*! From *tumanny* Albion!' England was referred to as 'Albion' and it had to be *tumanny* (foggy). If they were more informal, they might say, *Nu i kak Sherlock Kholms? So how is Sherlock Holmes?* By this point I really hated Sherlock Holmes.

These public exchanges were sometimes to be avoided, though, as they could result in picking up a 'tail' – not a KGB agent, but a random boy or man, of any age from about 10 to 70, wanting to follow me and ask me out on a date, or simply have a conversation with me while they walked alongside. These people were largely harmless and did not really care if I was a foreigner or not, they just wanted a girl to talk to. Once they realised I was a foreigner, they either disappeared, frightened of the consequences, or they dug in harder, determined to become a part of my life.

I could usually out-walk them or shake them off by going into a shop that said it sold ladies' underwear (even though the shop would often not turn out actually to have any ladies' underwear). This kind of thing could often be a hassle, though, as some people really had very little to do, and they could afford to hang out all day just seeing where I was going and if they could eventually wear me down. There was a time when two smirking goons in suits followed me up Nevsky Prospekt, the main street, for what seemed like 20 blocks. They were the *bandity* type, low-rent, small-time wise-guy types, probably chauffeurs or someone's bodyguards, bored on their lunch break. I tried getting rid of them by joining a queue for bread for half an hour. They waited outside the shop. I eventually shook them off by leading them deep into a store where I knew there was a large section of ladies' tights. I rounded on them and screamed, 'Attention! These bandits are following me!' They were chased out by several old ladies brandishing umbrellas, shouting, 'Shame on you!'

There were a few times in public spaces where I sensed a real kind of danger. If I walked home on my own after 11pm, whether the street was deserted or busy, a car would often appear alongside me.

They would wind down the window or even push the passenger door open. '*Devushka*. Girl. It's cold. Get in. The car is warm.' I hated these guys, because you couldn't get away from them and if you were walking along a long street in the freezing cold late at night, it wasn't as if you could turn into a courtyard or an alley. These kerb-crawlers were probably looking for a lady of the night or, more likely, a temporary, unpaid girlfriend. They were non-violent but insistent. I never knew whether to appease them – 'No, thanks, I'm fine' – or to berate them, so I learned to just ignore them and walk away decisively, wearing an angry face.

There was one time I did stop a guy in a car – because it was in broad daylight – and ask him to stop harassing me. He was driving alongside me in a slow traffic jam and there was no getting away from him. He kept winding his window down and hissing and whistling at me, making grotesque kissing noises. In the end, I stopped by the car and shouted into the window in perfect Russian, 'Go f— yourself, you arsehole piece of shit.'

He physically recoiled, an expression of horror on his face. Mortally offended, he began to shout at me that I was an immoral, disgusting woman who should be ashamed of herself. Then he wound up his window and accelerated for self-protection, shaking his head in despair at the state of the world. He clearly would not be seen dead with such a foul-mouthed harlot.

His reaction was hilarious. But I also knew this experiment was not to be repeated, especially not at night or alone. Being harassed was normal. Fighting back was not. I couldn't afford to attract attention to myself like that again.

* * *

One of the many barriers to my Russian being fluent enough to help me 'pass' and appear unassailable was my command of numbers – and in particular, the fluidity of numbers that you need when telling the time. It was an old Soviet trick used to identify foreigners: you simply mumbled 'What's the time?' at someone as you passed them on the street. If they glanced at their watch without flinching and shot back 'quarter past four' then you knew they were not foreign. If you couldn't answer immediately, the next question would be in English: 'Change money?' This wasn't a dangerous situation, but it was annoying, and people could be insistent about wanting to get their hands on a few dollars. It was Misha who taught me what to say, to get people to leave me alone. In Russian, there are a lot of ways of asking the time, but the easiest one is to ask, '*Kotory chas?*' *Which hour?* The word *chas* means *hour*, while the word for *wristwatch* is *chasy* – literally your *hours*. Asking the time, therefore, sounds very close to asking, 'Which watch?' One sarcastic answer to this is to say, '*Komy kak?*' – literally, *To whom, how?* As in: 'Who cares?' So if you translate these expressions word for word into English, you would say, 'Which watch?' 'To whom, how?' Misha found this hilarious, and it became a catchphrase. I wasn't totally sure we found this funny for the same reasons. But I appreciated having a phrase I could yell at people in the street without being accused of vulgar indecency. 'Which watch, you ask? I say, to whom, how!'

These phrases were vintage Misha. His main contribution to fostering what he called the 'friendship of the peoples' (a popular toast at the time) was the use of an expression which he considered to be quintessentially English: 'strictly directly.' He used this expression liberally, to mean 'immediately' or 'straightaway', and also when giving directions. If I ever asked him where somewhere was, he would reply in English, 'Strictly directly.' Whenever he said goodbye to me and ushered me home, he would shout after me, again in English, 'Strictly directly.' He also loved to say 'Home Alone', pronounced Soviet-style, 'Hom-yay Alon-yay'. The movie had been dubbed into Russian and was a source of fascination. Misha phrased this as a question almost every time he would telephone anyone, regardless of whether they were an English speaker or not: not so that he could ascertain whether they were home alone or not, but simply so that he could say 'Are you hom-yay alon-yay?' in a silly voice.

These Misha-isms were his attempt to try and understand something about a world that had been hidden from him for most of his life. He resented Western culture and was fascinated by it at the same time. He was more sceptical than most: he had no real desire to travel to the West, and no real interest in meeting other Westerners. Out of everyone around me, he expressed best what the contrast had been like over the last few years, suddenly seeing what had been suppressed: the consumer goods, the way of life, the freedom of expression, the casual joy in living. He was quietly angry about it a lot of the time but also accepting: whenever I tried to get him to talk about it on purpose, he would shrug and just say, *Tam . . . eto Tam. That's just how it is Over There.*

In public, I tried to behave how Misha would have wanted me to. He would berate me for smiling and laughing too much: 'Rearrange your face when you go into the street, Vivka. Everyone will know you are a foreigner. You smile too much. You can do that *tam*. Smile as much as you like Over There. But you can't do that here.'

He thought that it marked me out as bourgeois, or as he called it, being a 'yoghurt'. This was his word for 'Westerner.' He called

Westerners *yoghurty* (yoghurts) because he thought we looked as if we belonged in a commercial for yoghurt where everyone is really happy all the time. He claimed to be able to tell at a glance from someone's face whether they were foreign, and he would regularly point foreigners out to me discreetly as we walked down the street: 'Look, Vivka, another of your yoghurt comrades.' Whenever I asked him to explain more about his yoghurt theory, he would launch into long tirades about the non-existence of 'yoghurt' as a plausible foodstuff, claiming that *smetana* (sour cream) and *kefir* (a fermented milk drink) were the only dairy products that anyone needed, and that yoghurt was a bourgeois invention.

The more he talked about this, the more I thought about the faces of the happy *yoghurty* – of which I was one – walking down the street, their smiles in direct contrast to the guarded self-protection of Soviet citizens, the more I knew he was right. There was a lot about my home culture that was fake and 'for show' We were and always would be yoghurts.

* * *

I was generally getting by without too much aggravation about money. I had heard of British students in Moscow whose Muscovite host families wanted to charge for whatever they could. If they had a friend round to stay over, the family charged them ten dollars at breakfast. I struggled to imagine the sort of living quarters where you would have room to have a friend to stay over, but I could see that this situation was awkward. I kind of sympathised with the Russians: eggs were not cheap. But the etiquette was hard to navigate.

VIV GROSKOP

I had Russian and Ukrainian friends who asked for money just to see what would happen, students who asked if I could get hold of jeans for them, and other friends who really needed five dollars, a sum I lent a few times and which was sometimes repaid, sometimes not. I had other friends who never asked for anything and would go out of their way to be generous towards me in whatever way they could, whether it was by lending or giving me books, making introductions to interesting people, or cooking me food.

It was rare to see debit card or cash machines in Russia at this time, and where they did exist, I didn't trust them. Whatever money I needed, I had had to take it in with me. There were various stashes of money to last me through the year: cash in US dollars, travellers' cheques in US dollars and an emergency credit card. The cash was hidden in a lot of different places like my wash bag, in a tampon box – *poprobuitye Tampax, try Tampax!* – in various guidebooks: anywhere where, if it was found and I lost it, it wouldn't really matter, and there would still be some money left. From everything I had read in the Lonely Planet guide to the USSR, complete with updated section on the Commonwealth of Independent States, it was best to prepare in advance to be robbed.

Dima had mostly managed not to ask for money. Very possibly he still felt bad about all the Iron Maiden T-shirts I had bought him when he came to England. But one night a few friends of his came round and sat me down, looking up gravely over the *priyanniki* and *sushki* biscuits Katya had diligently put out. They explained that the smallest and weediest of them, Vitya, was up for military service. He needed 80 dollars for a doctor's note to sign him off with a bad back. I had heard horrific stories about military service: it was violent, abusive, brutal. Dima had a friend, Vanya, who had just come back from it. I had seen Vanya: he was quiet and difficult. Dima said his personality had completely changed. He didn't think Vitya would survive it. I said I'd think about it. What harm could it do? I gave the money even though I was thinking, 'I can pay for one person. But I can't pay for everyone he knows. So how is this going to end?' And what about Dima? When was his military service? It hadn't come up yet.

A week later the same group of friends sat me down again. Here we go, I thought. There will be a list of people who want 80 dollars. But, no, it wasn't that. Vitya had been mugged and had the money stolen. The bribe remained unpaid. He was contrite. 'It was as if I was walking down the street with a sign on my back saying, I have 80 dollars.' Looking at his face, I could tell he wasn't lying. He was too pathetic to be lying. He was just a kid. And now he needed another 80 dollars to replace the stolen money. Dima couldn't look at me. I realised it had been a mistake to give it in the first place.

I said I was really sorry but there was no more money. I'd had enough. 'Vipulya. Is there anyone else you can ask?' No. I had given the money out of guilt, but also out of a desire to belong and to not be a yoghurt. Or at least somehow to help. But I was not one of them and I never would be. Although maybe in another important way I had now become a bit more like them. I knew now what to say and how to say it. *Nyet. Nelzya. Obidno. No. It is forbidden. It is insulting.* All the *sovkovy* words I hated people saying to me, now I was saying them myself. They never raised the subject again.

*   *   *

It was the greatest compliment to be told you were *nash*, as in *nash chelovek* (our human). One of us. *Vash* meant *one of you* or *one of your lot*, as in *po-vashemu* (the way your lot do it), meaning *Western* or *Other*. I was often told on points of etiquette and language that certain things were not *po-nashemu* (our way).

Pride in whatever was closest or native to you was essential. For example, if you spent any time in St Petersburg, you would be expected to say that Moscow was a terrible, horrible city. No matter that the two are so different that you can't really compare them at all. It's like comparing Paris and New York. There were so many nuances that I didn't understand and that seemed mindlessly territorial.

Dima was particularly virulent about this kind of thing. He was livid enough that I had found myself a boyfriend who was not him. The fact that Bogdan was Ukrainian made it even worse. I don't think the precise nationality bothered him – Bogdan could have been from any former Soviet republic (or, maybe worse, from Moscow) and it would have disgusted him just as much. There was simply a sense that this 'rival' was 'not even Russian' and therefore the whole thing was an even greater insult.

Things became so tense with him that Katya moved me into her mother's apartment round the corner. We called her Babulya (Granny). The money from the school would help Babulya out and she'd like the company, Katya said. What I really wanted was independence, but I couldn't see how I was going to find my own place and still be officially registered. Katya understood: she knew that at home in England I lived on my own away from my parents. She arranged for her mother to live with me during the week and with her at weekends.

After I moved in with Babulya, I would come back to Dima's to visit Katya and Inessa. One night I went over after going to one of the band's gigs. After Katya and Inessa had gone to sleep in the other room, Dima and I sat up talking and smoking. Dima had taken the new living arrangements very badly and was sulking: 'All I can say is that you'd better not have that *khokhol* over to stay at Babulya's.' I gave him a look that said, 'And what are you going to do about it?' Which was a mistake.

I saw him begin to lunge at me and I stood up, but he was too fast. He grabbed my neck and held me by the throat, lifting me onto the tips of my toes. The span of his thumb and forefinger pushed my jaw upwards. Time stopped and turned to elastic. I could sense that this was happening in the space of a millisecond, but I could feel it also happening in slow motion, with every decision weighed up. *Can he hurt me? Would he hurt me? Does he mean it? Am I overreacting? Is he serious? He can't be serious.* And sensing in the same millisecond that none of these questions mattered, and *No* and *Get out* were the only things now. I pulled back, ducking and shrinking from him, and pushed one of the chairs loudly into the table. He wouldn't want to wake up his mother and sister. Numb and dazed, I stumbled to the coat rack by the front door and changed out of his mother's slippers into my boots. He stood in the doorway of the kitchen, glowering, breathing heavily. I put on my coat, opened the door, closed it and headed down the stairwell. I didn't take a last look at his face. I walked the two streets to Babulya's, hardly breathing in the freezing air.

I never went back to that apartment, and I never spoke to Dima again. I didn't tell anyone what had happened either, including my parents back home. Dima and I had a lot of friends in common, and

I didn't want them to have to take sides. I also didn't want to hear that I should have done something about it. I wasn't physically hurt, he hadn't left a mark, and it would be his word against mine. I didn't tell Katya and Inessa as it would have shamed them – either that, or they would have not believed me, and that would have broken my heart. I didn't tell Misha or Bogdan or the boys in the band, as I knew they would probably want to avenge me in some medieval way, or at least stage a confrontation. I just wanted to forget I had ever known Dima.

* * *

Getting away from Dima would require some big changes. I already had a new set of friends, even if they only came to the city for a few days a month. Now I needed a new home, and probably a new job. And I was going to have to do it on my own if I was going to avoid any more arguments.

Katya came round to Babulya's and I broke the news to her: it was very kind of them to try this arrangement but I really wanted to live alone. I would give my notice at the Vatson School of English and leave the following month. I tried to give her some money, but she wouldn't take it. She was stoic as ever and said she respected whatever I wanted to do. That conversation was the last time I heard someone call me Vipulya. Teeny tiny VIP was dead. Now I was what the Ukrainians called me: Vivka. Myself again. Or almost.

I embarked on a campaign to find somewhere to live, somewhere I would have my own room, maybe a *kommunalka*. I asked everyone I knew if they could help, and in explaining what I was looking for, I used the word *samostoyatel'no* (independent) a lot. In Russian, it literally means 'standing on your own'. I realised this was perhaps the closest word there was for 'private'; it really was some kind of privacy that I craved, a physical and mental space of my own. There was no Russian expression for 'privacy', and almost every space in any home was, essentially, communal whether it was a *kommunalka* or not. I had many friends who lived in families of four or five in two rooms plus a tiny kitchen and a bathroom. One room would be used as a sitting room, but everyone had sofas that were used as sofa beds: at night-time, the parents would sleep in the sitting room. I often felt clumsy and awkward in these spaces, knowing that the room in which a dinner was being served or a party being held was essentially someone's bedroom. I was prone to knocking things over or causing near-accidents. I was just not careful or respectful enough of property or of small spaces. Or maybe some subconscious part of me wanted to sabotage the relentless communality of it all.

It was Dryusha Green who came to the rescue. *Ya uznayu. Let me ask around.* He was a similar kind of person to Misha: enterprising, sociable, dynamic. People in our classes were friendly and supportive to us, and only occasionally overstepped the boundaries. Dryusha Green had once asked for Levi's, but as soon as I looked uncertain, he made a face that said, 'Can't blame a guy for trying.' Which was fair enough.

With his intervention, I unexpectedly entered the world of what Soviet culture called *blat*, or social capital. In the days of the USSR, a *blatnoy chelovek* (a person with *blat*, or clout) could get you products that were supposed to be available only on rations; they could find you a job; they could find you a flat without paying a bribe; they could game the system. *Blat* gave you a bit of freedom and a bit of leeway. When Russians translated this word into English, they called it 'profitable connections'. 'Or maybe you say old boys' network?' Call it what you wanted, I needed this *blat*.

And so Dryusha Green found Yuliya − a nurse friend of his wife's − who knew a teacher of poetry evening classes who knew Alexei, an 18-year-old boy whose parents had died a few years ago and had ended up with his own apartment which had a spare room. This was highly unusual: somehow he had flown beneath the radar of the authorities and not been re-housed. I met Yuliya's elderly teacher, and he assured me that he would take personal responsibility for this arrangement, that Alexei was taciturn but trustworthy. He was glad I would be keeping an eye on him.

And that is how I escaped. Now I was registered with the university instead of with the Vatson School of English. I was a student again instead of being a teacher. And instead of a host family who were possibly too interested in me, I had a flatmate who showed no interest in my life whatsoever. Alexei and I went on to exchange approximately ten words over the course of the next six months, an arrangement that suited both of us perfectly.

*   *   *

By the time I had to leave the Vatson School of English, I had actually become quite fond of my class. Ickersli believed that teaching a language was about covering 'the pill of learning with the jam of gaiety'. (I'm sure the rabbits, alive or dead, would agree.) In his books, the English language is taught in four stages with 500 words at each stage. In St Petersburg in the early 1990s, I had only ever seen the green book − Book No. 1 − which meant most of the people I knew had only ever been exposed to a maximum of 500 words in

English. No wonder we were struggling to understand each other. Correction: we had been struggling. (Pluperfect tense. Some of them were starting to ask for more grammar.)

Ever since the jam of gaiety had been introduced, however, in the form of asking the teacher nosy questions about her private life, the pill of learning had gone down a treat. The truth was, I was an unqualified and mostly lazy teacher, and there were days when I spent whole lessons just getting them to practise saying 'ship' and 'sheep', or 'paper' and 'pepper'. It was almost impossible for them to hear the difference, and it took up hours of class time.

Nonetheless, a few learners were actually making headway, and had started bringing in other materials for me to look at: album covers they wanted translating, magazines, old textbooks, computer manuals. It was sweet, but also overwhelming. Everyone was now revisiting their school lessons, and some brought in their old work-books to translate. But all the progress they were making in English didn't stop them from questioning mine. Ickersli's stranglehold was so tight that if ever I tried to correct someone or suggest another way of saying something, a student was very likely to say, 'But Ickersli says . . .'. In fact, over the months I spent in St Petersburg, Ickersli was brought to me repeatedly for clarification by children and adults alike. 'Ickersli says . . .' 'Can you explain what it means when Ickersli uses this word . . .' 'But Ickersli has another way of saying this . . .' '*A Ickersli* . . .' (but Ickersli . . .). I was allowed to interpret and translate the mighty words of Ickersli, but I was not allowed to question them or improve upon them. Ickersli's English was in a book and mine was not. So he must be right.

On the days when the conversation with my class switched to Russian, the questions about *Tam* were never-ending and always off-topic. Borys was also a great aficionado of such questioning. Shared preoccupations for him and the adult students included: 'Have you been to Liverpool? Do people in the UK like The Beatles? What is your father's monthly salary? Do you have *borsch* in England? How much does a vinyl album cost in England? How much does an electric guitar cost?' People would get very angry when I did not know the answer to things and would force me to guess.

'An electric guitar . . . I don't know . . . could be £100. Could be £2,000.'

'What do you mean? How can it be both?'

'I'm saying I don't know.'

'You must know. Can't you take a guess?'

'I am guessing.'

'Who has £2,000 to spend on a guitar?'

'I'm telling you, I don't know.'

'What about Levi's?'

And on it would go. In the absence of the internet, there was no choice but to do an impression of a walking encyclopaedia. It was a nightmare. But you couldn't blame them for wanting to know. They were kind and well meaning. We had all come a long way since the first week when they had tried to get me and the other teachers sacked.

On the last day of class, we had black tea and *sushki*, the weird rusks. I thought the *sushki* were a joke but it turned out they were part of a plot – surprise, surprise – to convince me of the *undeniable merits of sushki*. I announced over tea that we would speak no English today and everyone cheered. Snezhana revealed that she had been out one day with her *avoska*, the word for a 'just-in-case' bag you carried 'just in case' you happened upon a shop with an unexpected consignment of goods. She had seen a white mohair beret and bought it for me: 'For you to impress God's Gift, Son of God's Gift. With the beauty. And also it is cold.' There had been great concern amongst the class that I *did not dress up warmly enough against the cold*, and they had had a whip-round. The white beret was applauded, and then it was time to say *do svidanya*. Which, happily enough, doesn't mean goodbye. It means *until the meeting*.

* * *

I had plenty of other meetings of my own now. And even when Bogdan and the band weren't in town, I would hang out in some of their haunts. I was part of the music scene, even if I never quite knew with some people whether they liked me or they were just looking for someone to shout them a beer. After my last class at the Vatson School of English, I went to celebrate with Kuznetsov's girlfriend, Dina. She was someone who was, like me, a bit of a spare part. We weren't exactly groupies. But we also weren't in a band. We spent a lot of our time draping ourselves over moth-eaten sofas backstage, trying to look as if we were totally meant to be there. Mostly Dina and I got on. She was quirky and contrarian, and always wore an electric blue beret. She once walked away from a conversation with me because I said I wouldn't eat *kholodets* even if her mother made it for me. This is a legendary dish consisting of cold boiled beef in aspic: they translated it as 'jellied meat'. '*Obidno*,' she spat.

When we were getting on, we would sit and smoke cigarettes at the bar while her boyfriend talked 'business' with some bass guitarist or other. His gold tooth would flash in the light as he sold the dream of fame and fortune to the latest sucker. The guys in the bands lapped up his every word. It was a time of hope and possibility. And Kuznetsov was a man of energy and conviction, after all, wasn't he? Personally, I could already see that his plans rarely came to much. But he made it seem as if things might happen, that it was *all coming together*. And that if anything did happen, he, Kuznetsov, would, of course, be at the heart of it. (He often spoke of himself in the third person.) Sometimes the things he promised really did happen. This year, he was putting together the summer line-up for the much-vaunted Battle of the Bands. Everyone was looking ahead to the White Nights, the annual summer festival between May and July when there would be almost 24-hour daylight for weeks on end. Because it never got dark, people walked the streets all night, looking for parties. Colney Hatch already had bookings for some late-night outdoor gigs.

I stopped going to Kosmos completely. On the rare occasions I went back, it was only because Bogdan and the guys were on the bill. Even then, I felt uncomfortable there now. It was a hang-out Dima knew about and I didn't want to risk running into him. Instead, I started going to a place I loved on Griboyedov Kanal, a big empty nightclub space just off Nevsky Prospekt. I couldn't work out whether it was a derelict warehouse which had had a stage installed, complete with lavish red velvet curtains, or an old theatre which had had everything stripped out of it and so now looked like a warehouse. In any case, it only seemed to operate as a venue at the weekends. What happened there the rest of the time? I often wondered how people made decisions about how a space would be used and when it would be open. It all seemed so random. Trying to apply logic to the incoherence was becoming too exhausting. I told myself this was a negative, *yoghurty* way of looking at things: that if you just looked at things a little differently, you could see that this was a life filled with authenticity, charm and romance. Wasn't it?

This particular club was near my favourite church, the Church of the Saviour on Spilled Blood, Spas Na Krovi, along the canal from Kosmos towards the river and the Summer Gardens. Filled inside and out with thousands of pieces of mosaic work and with distinctive fairy-tale kaleidoscopic domes, this church was an architectural fever dream. The beauty of the place was uncomplicated. And yet, just like the nightclub-that-might-have-once-been-a-theatre, the church was famous for its reinventions. It was a morgue during the Siege of Leningrad in the 1940s and a potato warehouse in the 1950s, which was why some people called it Saviour on the Potatoes. Nothing in Russia was ever what it seemed, and everything had multiple identities which everyone took for granted, but did not explicitly explain. I was forever trying to accept that not everything here had to make sense. That if only I could reconcile all these contradictions in my mind, I would feel safer, fit in better and feel as if I belonged.

It really didn't help that my relationship to Bogdan was in some ways just as confusing as everything else. Was it the language barrier? Or was I just chasing after someone who wasn't that into me? My feelings for him were real and intense. But I didn't know whether he felt the same way about me. One night after a gig at the warehouse, I decided to confront him. We were walking to my place, but I couldn't convince him to stay over. He wanted to go to Misha's with the rest of the band. He got this way sometimes. 'Bodya, do you actually like me?' Again, unfortunately, this had to be phrased as *Am I indeed pleasing to you?* I thought that if he couldn't answer this properly or with sufficient enthusiasm, then I would just leave things be. *Chuchelo, obidno. You idiot scarecrow. You are insulting me. Of course you are indeed pleasing to me.* I didn't have a cold sore any more, so he kissed me properly. All confusion evaporated.

spring, n.
весна, vesna (Russian)
весна, vesna (Ukrainian)

After moving to Alexei's *kommunalka*, life got easier. In place of teaching, now I was studying. And I landed a work experience job at the offices of the St Petersburg Press, the English-language newspaper, where I hoped to do some writing. I filed reports on cultural happenings, loosely defined: everything from what was going on that week at the circus, where there was a visiting troupe of performing hedgehogs (I am not joking), to the ins and outs of the underground music scene, including, of course, a piece on Colney Hatch.

My registration with the university meant I was entitled to regular Russian lessons at the homes of two assertive young women who were best friends and PhD students. Svetlana and Ruslana took it in turns to school me in grammar, vocabulary and the Russian literary greats, and had strong opinions about my hair, make-up and clothes. They would give great long sermons about their philosophical beliefs and about the importance of 'culture', often with strangely resonant New Age asides. One day, when we were translating a Chekhov short story, Svetlana grabbed me by the shoulders, looked deep into my eyes and boomed, 'Vivka. Some people are vampires. And some people are radiators. You must always be a radiator.' This was a theory she explained often: that some people are incapable of doing anything but taking from others (the vampires). They take attention, love, money, time. Radiators are the opposite: they ask nothing of you and warm you with their presence. I applauded this theory, having just escaped the vampire that was Dima.

In the run-up to the long-awaited summer, my other teacher, although an unofficial one, was Misha. He taught me both Russian and Ukrainian, and swear words which I had to promise not to repeat because 'a girl cannot say these things'. He was my tutor in the difference between *mat* (profanity) and what I thought of as 'phone voice'. He was my dictionary, my translator of all Soviet customs, my therapist, and my hotline to whatever was happening with the band.

Misha had a constant parade of Ukrainians from back home traipsing through his flat, staying for a couple of nights or a few months, bringing slabs of *salo* (pork fat) wrapped in shiny brown paper, which they would eat in slivers perched on bits of chopped onion. Sometimes these Ukrainians seemed to be people he barely knew, although they were usually from his hometown. They all abided by an unspoken rule: if you come from a place and go to another place, you help anyone who is from your place.

Misha would make space for anyone who needed it, even if it meant he had nowhere to sleep himself. I had known him to sleep in the kitchen, his head on his forearms on the table. Once I went round to his flat to find the kitchen door had been taken off its hinges and balanced on a chair at either end. 'What is the door doing there?' I asked. 'Oh, that's where Vovka is sleeping at the moment,' he replied. Vovka was another random Ukrainian who came and went. He liked to slob about the place in boxer shorts and had legs like hairy anaemic hams. 'Aren't you worried he'll fall off the door?' I asked Misha. 'No, Vivka,' he said solemnly, 'He has beautiful legs.' Our new catchphrase was born: 'Everything will be fine. We have beautiful legs.'

Bogdan had started phoning every so often. Clearly Dima's presence had put him off before. But he still hated talking on the phone. Misha, on the other hand, very much did not hate using the phone and we continued to talk most days. I teased Misha on a regular basis about getting him a girlfriend and he would go beetroot-red and say, 'It's not my time, Vivka.' Then he would pull himself together, laugh and say, 'I don't need all that snivelling and sobbing.' He thought I snivelled and sobbed too much over Bogdan. He would say, *Polny relax, Vivka. Chill out.* I didn't see that it made much difference whether I was chilled out or not, seeing as Bogdan and I only saw each other for a few days a month anyway.

I continued to believe that I was 'madly in love' with this person, even though Bodya communicated with me far less than anyone – with the exception of Alexei, the perfect, silent, invisible flatmate. Alexei spent a lot of time listening to death metal on headphones. Our main interaction consisted of notes he would leave in the kitchen, tucked into the ripped wallpaper next to the phone, asking me to translate half-understood Sepultura and Slayer lyrics: *Shto eto znachet – BARN YOUR FLASH?* By which he meant *What does it mean – BURN YOUR FLESH?* I translated a lot of lyrics about medieval torture techniques.

I loved the peace and quiet of the flat. Now that I was free of my teaching timetable I realised the toll that it had taken: I just wasn't cut out to teach English. I got too involved with people, I took it all to heart, I was earnest and serious about making a difference but without any experience or common sense that would tell me how to actually make a difference. Now I had time to read and study and go to the theatre on my own instead. It was a better fit.

I leaned hard into new friendships, and acquired two girlfriends I saw at least once a week. Yana had a job as a manageress in a Finnish supermarket, the only place in the city where you could get imported Californian wine in glamorous carafe-style bottles, a large selection of which seemed to end up in her apartment. Then there was Yuliya – who I knew through Dryusha Green – who took me to cultural evenings where people recited Akhmatova, Mandelstam and Brodsky from memory, their eyelids fluttering. I had successfully escaped Dima. Now I had poetry, puns and as much Paul Masson rosé as I could drink. Yuliya, Misha and Yana were my new safety net. Finally, I could breathe.

* * *

The safety net met the ultimate stress-test when I caught dysentery. Yuliya came and sat with me in my apartment for three days in a row, dosing me with carbon powder. I was so miserable I thought I was going to die, and yet I still smiled when I thought about the fact that although I was very ill, I was not ill *and* having to face Dima. Yuliya attempted to cure the dysentery using incantations and reiki: *U menya tselebniye ruki' I have healing hands.* This may have been true, but I also had to pay for antibiotics from an American doctor on my otherwise-unused credit card.

As winter turned into spring, I was still living in my daydreams, namely in the perfect summer that I would have with Bogdan in Ukraine. One thing was worrying me, though. I wasn't sure how I was actually going to get to Ukraine. The train journey took the best part of two to three days, and it would be very difficult for me to travel alone. What if I got ill? What if someone asked me for a bribe? What if my bag got stolen? I had no experience of crossing the border and next to no experience of the train system. I decided that the solution was to do a practice run. Before the summer came around, I would take the train somewhere far away and make sure I knew what I was doing.

Fortunately – or, as it would turn out, unfortunately – I brought this up with Misha at his flat one day, when a man named Topik was staying with him. Topik was a slightly older Ukrainian who had a legendary status in the lives of both Misha and the band. He had been a few years ahead of Misha and the band at school, and had made a name for himself in his hometown as a 'businessman'. (This is one of my favourite Russian words of all time: *biznesmen*.) Topik was one of the guys who had appointed themselves a 'sponsor' of Colney Hatch, throwing 50 dollars their way every so often as some kind of pointless 'investment'. Topik was evasive about how he made his money, but he struck me as a straightforward wheeler-dealer: he had the charisma and the appetite for risk that would allow you to borrow a large sum of money, import a load of foreign goods, sell them off, pay the loan back and make a profit. I suspected that whatever he did was actually pretty boring, and this was why he resisted talking about it in detail. This was a common phenomenon at the time: glossing over the details of your working life because it was either dodgy or unimpressive. During Soviet times, professional and educational status were important because you couldn't gain status by amassing wealth. Now those old values were slipping away, and people weren't quite sure how to talk about themselves any more. For example, Misha went through a brief, improbable period as a lino salesman, but there was no way you could get him to talk about it.

Topik had a solution for my predicament. He needed to travel to Latvia to meet a business contact. He was heading for Riga, the capital, and then further west to the coast. I could go with him. *Genial'ny plan!' A genius plan! Na plyazh! Poekhali! We can go to the beach! Let's go!* He gesticulated wildly, brandishing all the verbs of motion. I weighed up the pros and cons. I more or less trusted Topik. He was a friend of Misha's and I had met his girlfriend, Tatiana, a tiny, model-like woman who resembled a miniature Sophia Loren. He was madly in love with her. She knew how to keep Topik's interest: she treated him disdainfully and would disappear for weeks on end without telling him where she was. I was pretty sure that Topik wouldn't try anything on while she drew breath. He treated me like a lot of male friends did at this time: as an honorary man, mostly because, being a foreigner, I had money. And it was because I had money that I was able to plan this trip. Topik was the only likely companion if I wanted to go to Latvia, because no one else I knew could afford to go there. The tickets for the night train from St Petersburg to Riga were booked: 16 hours.

The train journey was uneventful and took place mostly in darkness. We had our own cabin where we holed up, drank beer, talked incessantly, and dozed on and off. When we emerged at the other end, we walked around Riga for the day. I recognised the Art Nouveau style of the buildings. There were plenty in St Petersburg. But this was on a different scale: elaborate façades, fairy-tale turrets, ornamental sculptures on every block. In other parts of the city, there were rows of cute wooden houses. I didn't know anything about Denmark or Sweden and had never been anywhere like that, but this place *felt* Scandinavian to me, not Soviet: the architecture, the cobbled streets, the greenery. You could hear Russian spoken everywhere but also another language just as much: Latvian.

I had the strange feeling of wanting to be my British self again, a tourist in a European city. But just as quickly, I wanted to retreat into my Russian-speaking self and be more 'local', because I had got so used to trying to 'pass' in order to be safe. In Latvia, people looked at me as if I was foreign and left me alone without a second glance. Topik, on the other hand, was a target of barely-concealed hostility. People were brusque with him in bars, and in return he was condescending towards them. Although he was Ukrainian, he appeared to them to be Russian, and lots of Russians went to the Baltic coast to spend money, get drunk and to *polny relax*. It was just one of the reasons they were unpopular. Latvia was one of the three Baltic countries, alongside Lithuania and Estonia, that had strongly asserted its independence from Russia. I suddenly realised that travelling with Topik might be more of a liability than a benefit. I had come from a place where I always felt better protected if I was with a man, to a place where I would have been better off on my own as my unthreatening yoghurt self.

As it turned out, Topik had no business meetings in Latvia and just wanted to burn some cash. We took a train to the seaside and spent two weeks in a cheap hotel by the beach, sleeping a lot, drinking beer, smoking, reading books and talking rubbish. We shared a room with two single beds – pushed as far apart as I could manage, just in case. I liked him, but I soon established that he was something of a fantasist. He had ridiculous, grandiose plans to start nebulous businesses, coupled with the attention span of a gnat. He had money from somewhere or other, but I could sense that he was just spending it without knowing where the next chunk of cash would come from.

He could also be unhinged. On one of our last nights in Jūrmala, I woke up in our hotel room to find him sobbing like a child, tears streaming down his cheeks, clearly more than slightly drunk. 'Topik, calm down. What happened?' It took a lot of gulping and shuddering for him to be able to talk. He had woken up in the middle of the night and been unable to sleep, so he went out to a bar and got drunk. He got talking to a woman and ended up paying to have sex with her. This was unexpected. But, I realised, not entirely surprising.

The paid sex, though, was not what he was crying about. While he was having sex, he had taken off an Orthodox crucifix that he wore on a string around his neck. He did not want to be disrespectful, so he had put it by the bedside. He left the woman's place and walked back to the hotel. When he got back, he realised the crucifix was gone, but he was too drunk to remember where he had come from so he couldn't go back to get it. The crucifix was lost forever.

He started crying again. He should never have gone with this *prostitutka*. This was a punishment. A curse had been put on him. This was the spirit of Tatiana, getting her revenge. 'You won't tell her, will you, Vivka?' 'No,' I promised, 'I won't.' I rolled my eyes. 'Now go to sleep and stop being a big baby. We will get you another crucifix at the market tomorrow.' Now and again he would whimper in his sleep and I would say loudly, *Obidno. You are insulting me.*

When we got back to St Petersburg, I didn't tell Misha about the prostitute and the crucifix. I knew he would only blame himself for vouching for Topik. Plus, I thought that by not talking about it, I could pretend it hadn't happened. Topik popped up every few weeks at Misha's flat and once, randomly, he came round to mine, shame-faced. Could I lend him five dollars? Or maybe ten, if I could spare it? He returned the money – in roubles, annoyingly, not dollars – within a week and after that, he vanished. At least my instincts were right sometimes: he was no big-shot businessman after all. This wasn't much consolation, though. I was just so exhausted by crazy people.

* * *

The closer it got to booking the tickets to Ukraine, the less convinced I became that I could make the trip on my own. I didn't need to go alone – I just needed to go with someone who was not crazy. The best thing would be if Misha could take me, but it was a favour too far even for him. 'I can't take you to Ukraine. I am busy. Roza is travelling from Moscow. She will take you to Ukraine.' 'Who is Roza?' 'My former teacher. She is from Moscow. But now she lives in Krivoy Rog.' This was Bogdan and Misha's hometown, my eventual destination.

'But I don't know her. It's a long journey.'

'So you will get to know her on the train.'

'What does she teach?'

'English.'

'But you don't speak English.'

'She's not a great teacher.'

'In what sense are you "busy"?'

No answer. 'Misha, I'll pay for your ticket. Don't you want to go home?'

'Vivka, *obidno*. I'm just busy, OK?'

The real reason why Misha wasn't taking me himself . . .? Well, that was complicated. The truth was, maybe he didn't really want to make it easy for me to see Bogdan. Or maybe on a train journey of that length, we would both be forced to think about the fact that it was a bit odd that we were such close friends. I half-knew and half-ignored these possibilities, and certainly didn't fully admit any of this to myself. I got him to consider a compromise: he would take me as far as Moscow and hook me up with the mysterious Roza. He said he'd think about it.

As summer finally arrived and my departure for Ukraine approached, my birthday fell in early July, shortly before I was due to leave. I was turning 21. The Ukrainians from the band were not going to be in town because they were preparing for their summer tour, but I still wanted to have a big party. This was my once-in-a-lifetime opportunity to celebrate in 'the Venice of the north' and I decided to book a boat trip around the canals. I hadn't dug into my travellers' cheques yet, and so I splashed out on a cake made at the famous Sever bakery store on Nevsky Prospekt. I also bought the ingredients to make open caviar sandwiches, which proved very inconvenient to transport. I invited everyone I knew: students from my class, my 'radiator' Russian teachers, Yana and Yuliya, Misha and some of his hangers-on. They all turned up with gifts of sparkling wine, books, chocolates, sweets.

Just as we were about to set sail for the strictly-timed and strictly-budgeted one-hour trip around the canals, a man bearing a remarkable resemblance to Topik appeared at the quayside, clutching something furry and wriggling inside his jacket. 'Misha. What's going on?, I thought Topik was out of town?' 'That's not Topik. That's his brother.' Topik's brother, who was identical to Topik, only slightly older and taller, bowed low in greeting, or at least as low as he could manage, considering that he was clearly carrying something awkwardly. 'You must be Vivka. Topik has sent me in his place. I brought you a present. Happy birthday.' He attempted to hand me the boisterous contents of his jacket: it was a puppy. A ridiculously cute Labrador puppy. I recoiled. I knew nothing about dogs, but this one seemed as if it was only a few weeks old. I tried to look grateful. 'That's so kind of you, but I am travelling back to England in a few weeks and . . .'. There was only one word that would shut down this gift in the right way: *nelzya*.

Topik's brother pursed his lips and tucked the puppy reluctantly further into his jacket. 'Well, think about it, Vivka . . .' he said half-heartedly. 'Topik really wanted to give you a special gift.' I gave Misha a look. He had got me involved with these people. He owed me. The puppy had decided it: Misha would accompany me to Moscow to meet Roza. Topik's brother, meanwhile, ate a lot of caviar sandwiches and made a very long face when he had to leave the boat, still clutching a puppy under his jumper.

summer, n.
лето, leto (Russian)
літо, lito (Ukrainian)

Finally it was July 1994 and I had a date with destiny. It was going to take three train journeys to get to central Ukraine. First we had to go to Moscow. Then 12 hours from Moscow to Kiev. Then eight hours to Krivoy Rog. Or maybe it took longer? I'm not sure. It would certainly end up feeling like much longer. I had to get through the trip to Moscow with Misha first. We took the train together and stayed with people he knew for a few days. I didn't want to stay with these random people, but I had given up caring about stuff like this. I just wanted to get to Bodya.

Roza materialised, and Misha went back to St Petersburg. Roza and I walked around the Kremlin walls at dusk, ate ice cream in Red Square and had our photos taken in a passport photo booth, making silly faces. My initial impression of her was positive. She was intelligent and full of curiosity. Yes, I could sense a bossy streak which was rarely far from the surface. But she seemed fun. She had slightly buck teeth that were a little bit too big for her mouth. She was ready to smile, quick to criticise and never stopped talking.

One of my favourite things about Roza – eventually probably the only thing I really liked about her – was that she was supposedly an English teacher, but she really did not speak any English at all. This did not surprise me, since Misha's English was a mixture of made-up phrases, mistranslations and half-understood advertising slogans. I tried to say 'strictly directly' and 'hom-yay alon-yay' to Roza as a joke several times, before realising that these phrases clearly did not originate from her teaching. Without having even Misha's sayings in common, she was just another person I had somehow ended up with and really knew nothing about.

*   *   *

I slept well on the train from Moscow to Kiev, and the starched white bedding was comfortable and clean. Or so it seemed at the time. The illusory state of the train's hygiene was to become salient in the weeks ahead. It was annoying to be with Roza, and yet annoyingly comforting at the same time. It was better than being alone. She kept up a steady rant about the poetry of Anna Akhmatova, the drawbacks of instant coffee compared to Turkish coffee, and the differences between the winters in Ukraine and St Petersburg, as well as constantly canvassing my views about what sort of boyfriend Misha would make and whether there were many men like him in my country.

Over the course of the next few dozen hours in a lurching train carriage with no means of escape, it became painfully obvious that she had decided to play matchmaker. I didn't quite know what to make of this conversation, as I judged Misha to be my only true friend and the one person I could really trust. Of course, I was in love – or very possibly in carnal lust – with Bogdan, and I was blinded with idiotic romantic notions whenever I thought of him. But Misha was a sensible person. I had literally trusted him with my life on occasion, in ways in which I would never actually trust Bogdan. Boyfriend material, though? No way. Misha was like the brother I had never had. Which was why it made sense that he had entrusted me to this annoying governess-like woman: she was a pain but she was also – as Misha would have put it himself – *necessary travelling companion.*

I don't remember us staying over anywhere in Kiev. It must have been a direct connection. I spent more time in Kiev a few years later. On this trip we just wanted to get south, fast. I wanted the time to pass quickly, but Roza seemed to want to make the most of things. On all train journeys, Roza drank tea incessantly – or rather, she had to have a steaming hot full cup of tea in front of her at all times, but hardly ever actually drank it. She considered the bottomless provision of hot tea to be one of the main perks of this journey – which I was pretty sure I had paid for, the details of the ticket acquisition being, like so many transactions, a bit hazy – and she was going to exploit it to the max. I didn't ever buy train tickets myself. ('Vivka, no! They will deceive you! They are all thieves and criminals. Better that I do it.') As a foreigner, you would be expected to pay more and you might be asked for a bribe of some kind. It made a lot more sense for me to pay for everyone travelling at local prices than to pay for my own ticket at foreigner prices.

In 1991 'Soviet Railways' in Ukraine had become 'Ukrainian Railways', as the country became independent. The way it was run was symptomatic of the mixed messaging of the time: it was supposed to be Ukrainian, but really it was still Soviet in all but name. You couldn't call anything first, second and third class under communism because it might mean that some people were better than others – you had to give it different names. So first class was called 'SV', which meant you could travel alone in your own compartment or with one other person. You got special attention from the *provodnik* (male train attendant) or *provodnitsa* (female train attendant). The next class down was 'coupé', one along from the first-class compartments we had booked, and usually meant you had other people with you in your carriage. Then there was the supposedly unthinkable *platskart* – third class – which meant you got a bunk, but the bunks were all open to the same carriage. (Beyond this there was a fourth class – upright seats. Which doesn't sound awful until you realise your journey is more than 12 hours and overnight.)

I walked up and down the whole train trying to work out the distinctions between these classes, and whether it really was as dangerous to travel *platskart* as everyone said. Really, I couldn't see that much difference. I had travelled *platskart* with Russian friends once or twice, and the bonus was that you got a lot of food: strangers just shared everything they brought with them. On a journey of this length, though, I really didn't need this kind of generous sharing experience. I was nil by mouth, trying to do as many hours as possible without going to the toilet. The toilets were the same for all classes of travellers, and universally terrifying. If you were lucky, it was a glorified bucket attached to the floor. If you were unlucky, it was a hole in the floor demarcated by two steel plates either side, the train tracks below cascading past in a blur at the bottom of the chasm beneath you. There was also a handrail to cling on to, for dear life.

* * *

As we hurtled south from Kiev, the further we travelled, the warmer it got. Summer was already here. Finally, I had come to a place where the sun was going to shine. For the first time in months, I felt as if I could breathe. The whole of me unknotted. There was a knock at the door of our compartment: the *provodnitsa. Khotite li chai' Do you want tea*? Roza looked at me sharply to stop me from speaking to the lady. Along with so many other friends in that post-Soviet era, she could never warn me enough of the dangers of speaking to strangers. She didn't want the *provodnitsa* rootling through our passports and asking for a hard currency back-hander once she knew there was a foreigner in the compartment. I had made this mistake on other occasions, and stood awkwardly for what felt like hours on end while some bureaucrat gorged himself on the rare spectacle of a foreign passport.

Roza would handle the refreshments. The *provodnitsa* had a massive, ancient samovar in her little cubby hole at the end of the carriage, and made a great show of decanting tea from a teapot and topping it up with boiling water, before transferring the glasses of tea to a precariously-borne tray to convey them, Mrs Overall-style, to our carriage. I could never quite get used to these *stakany*, which resembled British half-pint glasses, inserted into *podstakan-niky* – ornate silver holders – so that you didn't burn your hands. They seemed like something out of the 18th century. I used to think, *What's wrong with a mug*? But now I had trained myself out of thinking such things, and learned to ignore the fact that the tea against the glass always burned my lips.

As the Bulgarian author Georgi Gospodinov writes in his novel *Time Shelter,* our memories of the past are captured 'in scent and in light'. I can still smell and feel that train, the light a mix of harsh and artificial, and bright, bright sunlight; the slightly corroded tang of Soviet metal. The surprising fresh whiteness of the starched sheets that were handed over so that you could make up your bed. The rouged cheeks and heavy green eyeshadow of the cadaverous train attendant. And at last now, finally: the yellow glow of the sunflowers lighting up the windows. *Sonyashniki* in Ukrainian, *podsolnechniki* in Russian. The sunflowers meant we were close to our destination. They looked unreal, a hologram screened on a loop in the window of the train carriage. I flipped myself over on the bunk, turned my face to the window and laughed with delight. Sunflowers, summer and sun. And soon – soon! – I would be with *him.* There were some things I didn't need to pretend to be cool about. He was one. Why shouldn't fields of sunflowers be another?

Ukraine has 6.5 million hectares of sunflowers. A quarter of all agricultural space is given over to them. Ukraine was then, and still is, after Russia, the world's most important sunflower-growing country. Even without knowing the numbers and this impressive world ranking, I could look out of the window and see for myself that this was the home of the sunflower. So many of them, and so perfect and unsubtle that they were pure joy. They made me laugh in the same way that I had first laughed when I looked up and saw how comically beautifully Bogdan was.

We were passing through the most important cultivation region, a place I tried to pronounce over and over in my head: Dnipropetrovsk.

There were strange words and slight linguistic differences I needed to learn, terms close together in sound and meaning but with subtle changes. I had learned that you could say any of these words easily as long you really slowed them down. *Pod-sol-nech-ni-ki*. D-ni-pro-pet-rovsk. I had got used to all these colliding consonants that you stumble over as a native English speaker: 'dn', making you sound as if your nose is blocked; 'vsk', popping up in the middle of a word as if you're calling a cat in for dinner.

In Russian, *podsolnechniki* were *the flowers that grow under the sun*. In Ukrainian, *sonyashniki* had a more earthy name, less literal, more simple: *flowers of the sun*. By now, I loved the sound of these words in my mouth. They reminded me of the weird collision of consonants in my own name, a word which always needed to be spelled out. Groskop, the name that I thought and hoped meant that I was also from this place. *Sonyashniki*. Dnipropetrovsk. Except almost no one called Dnipropetrovsk with a Ukrainian 'i' then. They called it Dnepropetrovsk with an 'e', the Russian way.

As we gawped at the sunflowers, I stripped off down to a vest, bundled up my jumper into my bag and pulled my hair back with an elastic band. I made my bag into a pillow at the foot of the top bunk and lay with my feet at the window end, the back of my head resting on my hands, and watched the kaleidoscope moving to the rhythm of the train. I closed my eyes and let them flutter open occasionally to see if the sunflowers were still there. Of course they were. I sighed deeply. This was the life. This was *my* life. Warmed by the sun, filled with light, in love. Unaccountable. Or at least that's how it would be all summer. I practised saying it again in my head, faster and faster, using the rhythm of the train: Dne-pro-petrovsk. Dne-pro-petrovsk. If I practised enough, I could say it faster. The accent sounded plausible. Nearly. So nearly there.

* * *

Arriving in Krivoy Rog in the July heat was disorientating. I had been warned it would be warmer down south, but I was not expecting this. I never thought anywhere in the former Soviet Union would be hot, no matter what anyone said – it just seemed wrong. But here, it was as if there was a haze over everything, a film of dust covering the roads, the buildings, my skin, my hair. This was a dry heat unlike anything I had ever felt. Every train that arrived at the station unleashed more clouds of dust. I had never been anywhere like Turkey or Greece, but this was what I thought that would feel like. I felt as if I had ended up somewhere beyond where I had intended, like I'd stepped off the map.

I was used to travelling to work at 6am on a tram in minus temperatures that seemed to chill your clothes themselves and shrink your bones. Heading out into that cold for months on end had a numbing effect: you shut yourself off, you didn't make eye contact with anyone else on public transport, you kept your breathing shallow to stay warm. Here the effect was the opposite. Despite the dust and the dryness of the air, I could feel my bones being warmed, expanding. There was no humidity and no bright sunshine, just arid heat. When the train pulled into the station at the end of a journey that had started almost three days ago, I felt both relieved and exhausted.

It wasn't just the weather that felt different to St Petersburg; the whole atmosphere had changed. The difference was subtle, but I could feel it immediately on the train platform: there were fewer rules here, and in a good way. It was more of a mess, but you did not feel so observed. It was hard to fight the Western assumption that all these places should be the same because they had all been 'Soviet' or 'behind the iron curtain', but I was now in a place 1200 miles away. How could that possibly feel the same? Of course it couldn't. A little further south and you could cross the sea straight to Istanbul.

We stumbled out of the carriage, lugging the boxes of stuff that Roza's friends had sent with us. 'God, what is in here?' I cursed in English under my breath. I had trained myself to even speak to myself – under my breath, in my thoughts, in my dreams – in Russian. But this train journey and the stream of constant commentary . . . it had got to me. My English self was fighting back.

As we lugged them off the train, Roza's friends' boxes rattled, the contents threatening to escape their flimsy cardboard casings unless you supported them along their gaping seams. Glassware. Sodding *jam*. And pickled gherkins. And probably alcohol. Once you were set to go on a journey anywhere, people loaded you down with stuff destined for friends and family members. It was too hot to be lugging other people's pointless stuff from Kiev to this place in the middle of nowhere. I coughed as another dust cloud seemed to settle around us, dumping the box of pointless items as gracefully as I could and rifling through my bag for my asthma inhaler.

I hitched my shirt up and glanced over, annoyed, at Roza. She was wearing a T-shirt of mine that was lighter than the top I was wearing and better suited for this weather. She was tiny. I was not. And it was way too big for her, although it did look cute, I had to admit. Somehow over the course of the journey from Moscow, this perfect long-sleeved summer T-shirt – pretty much the only perfect one I had in the meagre wardrobe I had brought over from home in England, carefully designed to last through several seasons – had morphed from being my T-shirt to being hers. I had ended up giving away so much of my stuff, mostly by accident. Here's how it would go.

'Oh, Vivka, I love your T-shirt. It's amazing.'

'Thanks.'

'We don't have anything like that over here.'

'You don't?'

'Oh no. Look at the quality.'

'Thanks.'

'I bet you have lots of things like that in all the shops. Many of those kinds of things.'

'Yes, I guess we do.'

'That must be nice.'

A long pause.

'Do you want this T-shirt?'

'As a gift?' (The person would always check they were not going to have to pay for this exchange.)

'Er, yes, of course.'

'Oh, wow, thanks! Are you sure?'

Well, no, I'm not really sure about any of this, but here we are, and here I am, wearing what is basically a thermal vest designed to be worn underneath jumpers in the winter to keep me warm and sod-all use at 35C – but it's the only sleeveless top I have left because I have given the rest of my stuff away out of foreigner guilt. Bez problyem, I always said. No problem.

'Nice shirt,' called a bearded man to Roza. 'Denis!' Another person I didn't know and who had no connection to me. 'So you must be Vivka the Foreigner.' 'Yes, I am Vivka the Foreigner.'

Denis had come to meet us off the train. Meeting a train at the station was a whole art. So often, it would mean that you should intend to spend the whole day at the station, turning up expectantly at the platform for each train until the right one finally arrived. Denis chatted away, asking questions about my provenance and life purpose, while Roza counted up the boxes, and went back and forth to our compartment to check we hadn't left anything behind.

Denis was a mate of Misha's, of course. He seemed nice. But there was only one person I had come here to see. *Roza, gde Bogdan? Where's Bogdan?* I thought he was coming to get me. I scoured the crowds on the platform, people pouring off the train, people meeting them, people selling stuff, people sniffing around Roza's jangling boxes to see if there might be a bargain or something you could easily nick. 'Who's Bogdan?' asked Denis. 'Bogdan will come along,' Roza replied. This sounded alarmingly vague to me all of a sudden. 'What do you mean, "will come along"?' She had used *podaidyot*, a sketchy verb of motion in the future tense which means something like *he'll pop along*. 'Is he collecting me or not? Should I wait here? Where should I wait?' 'Don't wait anywhere. Come with us. Come on, let's go.' Denis shrugged.

I considered getting angry and throwing a tantrum. Or crying – because that was what I wanted to do. But I swallowed hard and reminded myself to be grateful to these people who were effectively keeping me safe and looking after me. As I hauled my stuff along the platform, still fielding Denis's many questions, I cast my eyes forlornly up and down the platform. 'How many trains arrive a day from Kiev?' I asked. 'Probably five? Or ten. I don't know. Maybe one,' Denis yelled over the noise. There was no way Bogdan had come to meet me off this train. How would he know which train anyway? Why hadn't I thought this through?

This was supposed to be my Summer of Love travelling around the most beautiful parts of southern Ukraine, breathing in the sunshine from fields of sunflowers and basking in the glow of passion with my boyfriend on tour with his band. It was supposed to be cool and exciting. Instead I was stuck with a bespectacled man with zero knowledge of the post-Soviet rail network and a tiny garrulous woman who had stolen my T-shirt. Worse, the three of us were weighed down by hundreds of clinking bottles of homemade condiments. This was not the romantic Ukrainian dream I had been promised. I had to find Bogdan fast.

* * *

Unfortunately, Roza had other priorities. And as soon as we had lugged our bags and all the boxes into her flat, she waved off Denis and commenced her mission: to get a dose of fermented rye into me. For some time, a number of people had tried to convince me of the merits of *kvas*. This is a traditional cereal-based fermented beverage made from rye bread or rye flour and malt. There were regional variants of this antiquated drink everywhere. And everywhere you went in the former Soviet Union, they would tell you that their *kvas* is 'the original Coca Cola'. This is a joke in the same camp as 'to hell with Bill Clinton' and 'Moscow is a big village', in the sense that every time anyone said it, they acted as if they were the first. The fact was, everyone knew it was nothing like Coca Cola. To say that *kvas* is like Coca Cola is to say that an apple is like a Mars bar. I suppose it is similar in that it is nominally a recreational non-alcoholic drink – except, of course, it's not non-alcoholic. It's around 1% or 2%, so it falls into the realm of post-Soviet drinks which are technically alcoholic but are not considered to be. Beer was also considered such a drink. I had had many boring arguments with the guys in the band about whether or not Obolon – a 5% Ukrainian lager – was a 'soft drink'.

When someone tries to convert you to *kvas*, they don't just say, 'Why don't you try this drink and see if you like it?' Instead they say, 'This drink has extraordinary properties. It guarantees long life. It will make you strong and beautiful.' But it wouldn't stop there. '*Kvas* is a national drink. You cannot understand this country or anything about it unless you drink *kvas*.'

Sitting me down in her pristine kitchen, Roza began her battle to get me to consume it, while I tried with all my might to persuade her to contact Bogdan.

'Roza. I have Bogdan's address. We should just go there. I don't want to bother you by staying here.'

'You're not bothering me. You need to rest after the journey.'

'But I think he'll be worried. He knew I was due to arrive by now.'

'Misha will let him know we've arrived.'

'But how? They don't have a phone.'

'Misha will let him know.'

'Can we not just go there?'

'No, no, we can't, Vivka, you don't understand. His parents might not like it. I don't know them. Misha doesn't know them.'

'But they're expecting me.'

I managed to persuade her to call Misha, who was back in St Petersburg. They argued for a long time, with Roza suggesting that maybe it would be better if I just spent the whole visit with her, and Misha trying to talk her down from this position, with me listening in, horrified but pretending not to understand too much.

I looked around. Her flat was, at least, hospitable. In all the time I had been there she was one of the only people I had ever met who had her own space and clearly lived in it alone most of the time. Maybe she wasn't as daffy as she seemed. To be fair, there were worse pseudo-kidnappers in the world than Roza, with her well-meaning pixie face. She put the phone down, an enormous red 1980s contraption with a dial. She smiled at me brightly and said, 'After you drink my *okroshka*, you will not want to leave.' My heart sank.

Along with *kvas*, Roza had been talking about *okroshka* all the way down here. It was her signature dish, a legendary family recipe, the crème de la crème. *Okroshka* is a cold summer soup not unlike vichyssoise. It usually has spring vegetables, radishes, cucumbers, dill, potatoes and spring onions in it, and is white and green in colour. The liquid component of it is made with – you guessed it – *kvas*.

By this point in the year, I had eaten so many things that were alien and even unpleasant to me that nothing really fazed me, and I was capable of pretending to like almost anything. I tried so, so hard to make it look as if I was enjoying it, but *okroshka* defeated me. Imagine a salty, cold, milky soup which tastes like a vinegary mix of cider and kombucha. The texture is fizzy and bubbling, like apple juice that has gone off.

Roza could see that I hated it, and she was angry. I fought back tears. I had got myself into an impossible situation: hostage to vats of fizzy *okroshka*, all bubbling with bits of radish and gherkin. I didn't know where Bogdan was, or if he even knew that I was here.

I started thinking that I was now trapped in this apartment. All I had wanted was one summer with him. Was that really so much to ask? I felt comprehensively sorry for myself, and big hot tears plopped down into the godawful soup.

* * *

It took two days, but Bogdan found me. By the time he tracked me down to Roza's flat, I was exhausted, fed up, and very slightly scared. I hardly ever got homesick for England, but by then I just really wanted to go home. Roza had invited some neighbours round for tea. Or rather, round for enforced *okroshka*. They gawped at me and asked the usual questions about The Beatles. Even though this was a city of 600,000 people, I asked them if they knew Bogdan. They didn't.

This kind of behaviour did not feel welcoming to me. It felt old-school Soviet. People reverting to the default: owning the foreigner, showcasing her, treating her like a pet. I felt bad for thinking these things too, though, as I was also aware that I was lucky to know people like Roza. She had looked after me and made sure I had made it to Krivoy Rog safely. But now she wouldn't let me go, and she also still wouldn't stop talking at me. Confronted with this torrent of words, she had also talked at me by this point for almost a week straight, keeping up a constant stream of consciousness about everything from the unassailable greatness of Pushkin ('I know you have your Shakespeare but. . .') and the scandal of the *fiktivny brak* (fictitious marriage) between singers Philip Kirkorov and Alla Puga-cheva ('she is 45 and he is 27, *eto ne normal'no, this is not normal, eto prosto skandal, it is simply a scandal*'), to the correct way to eat dumplings ('vinegar only – sour cream is objectionable') and the impossibility of me understanding irregular verbs of motion ('you are a foreigner, it will never come naturally to you'). The only verb of motion I was interested in was the one known as a perfective: the one where the action of the motion has already been accomplished and I have completed my travel and been reunited with the person for whom I undertook this interminable trip.

Motion between Moscow and Krivoy Rog had been achieved. But since then, I had been stuck on Roza's rickety put-me-up, prevented from finding my boyfriend and fed a relentless diet of *okroshka* and celebrity gossip. When Bogdan finally knocked on the door, we stood on the threshold and held each other for a long time. There was nothing sexual in it: just pure longing, relief and a sort of sweetness. He was a good person and a kind person, and he had been through it, searching everywhere for me.

It had been maybe a month since I'd seen him, and he seemed different here on his home turf: softer and less guarded than he was in the city back in Russia. He was usually embarrassed by displays of emotion, and was self-conscious about making a fool of himself over a foreign woman. It was such a cliché, after all. I was glad he was that way. I didn't want him to fawn over me. But on this occasion, we didn't care how it looked.

There had always been a part of me thinking that it was me who was in love with him, and that he would never really be in love with me back. But now I allowed myself to think, 'Oh. Maybe we are in love *with each other*.' Before, I had always made myself not believe it because it would have made me too happy.

I rarely saw him angry, but I could tell he was close to losing it with Roza. They were gabbling at each other in a mix of Russian and Ukrainian. The past few days had been ridiculous for him. He had scoured the whole city trying to find me. He had been to the station five times. He had worried that something terrible had happened to me. I could tell just from his face that he really had been anxious and had not known what to do. I was confused; he said he had Roza's phone number all along, and he had called the big red telephone from a payphone in the street. Multiple times. But Roza either hadn't answered or hadn't told me. I had heard the phone ring so many times, and she always said it was Misha. Now I was becoming livid too. 'So you called?' I said, my eyes filling up.

Roza cut me off, shrugged her shoulders and said that I had been very well looked after and what's the hurry, the two of us were going to have the whole summer together. 'Who can blame me for wanting to hold on to our foreign guest? Now, Vivka, come along. Are you sure you don't want to stay with me?' *Finally the truth*, I thought to myself huffily. *Well, this trophy has had enough of being exhibited.* Roza wasn't giving up, and started quizzing Bogdan on his parents' flat, whether there was really room for me, and whether it was really in a suitable part of town where I would be sufficiently 'cosy'. *Pofig mne uyutno*, I thought to myself. To hell with your 'cosy'. 'Let's get out of here,' Bogdan said in a low voice. We prepared to make our escape as soon as Roza went into the kitchen, determined that he would also sample the legendary *okroshka*. 'It's OK,' he shouted through. 'It's very kind of you but my mother is cooking and she is waiting for us.' A mother's cooking was the trump card. Roza held me tight, weeping slightly, and grabbed my cheeks as if I were a chubby Italian toddler. I thanked her as sincerely as I could muster. Despite how weird things had got, she was not a bad person. On the street I clung to Bogdan as if I never wanted to let him go.

'She kidnapped you.' Yes, I agreed solemnly. *Chyort poberi*, he said under his breath, kicking a stone across the road as he uttered the curse. *May the devil take her.*

* * *

As we headed down the street, we were so wrapped up in each other that we could barely walk for tripping over. I hadn't been outdoors much at this point as Roza had largely kept me in her kitchen. But once we got into the street, I could sense that despite the different climate, the streets had an eerie familiarity. It was just the same as the *spalny rayon* – the 'sleeping area', the commuter belt suburbs of St Petersburg or Moscow. The outline of hundreds of blocks of flats stretched into the distance.

Krivoy Rog (Krivih Rih in Ukrainian) was – and still is, 30 years on – an industrial centre, the largest city in central Ukraine and the longest urban development in Europe, built along an iron seam of more than 62 miles. I took it all in like a tourist, looking for clues and differences. The colour of the concrete, the brick, the light fittings, the shape of the railings . . . they were always the same. They were standard. It was as if someone was always trying to tell you that you could travel as far away as you liked, you would always be trapped within the same universe.

It reminded me of *The Irony of Fate*. This 1976 film took the idea that every town in the Soviet Union looked exactly the same and ran with it. The whole plot rests on the idea that it wouldn't matter whether you owned an apartment in Leningrad or in Moscow, it would look identical, both inside and outside. It was possible, so the argument went in the film, that you could even unlock the 'same' apartment in another city. 'Standard apartments with standard locks.' You would likely share your address with dozens of others in other cities across the USSR.

In the movie, four old friends are celebrating the impending New Year in Moscow with a traditional visit to the *banya* (sauna), where they all get steaming drunk. One of them, Pavlik, is due to fly to Leningrad first thing the next day to get home in time to celebrate New Year's Eve with his wife. Another friend, Misha, has big news: one of the reasons for them celebrating so hard is because he has announced that he's getting married. When Pavlik and Misha both pass out, the other two friends can't remember which of them is supposed to get to the airport and catch a flight. They decide it must be Misha. So they put him, half asleep, on the plane. Still drunk upon arrival in Leningrad, Misha hails a taxi and gives the driver his home address: Third Builders' Street, Block 25, Flat 12. When he gets there, the key fits the lock and he falls into bed. Only to wake up with a woman he doesn't know, in an apartment that isn't his, in the wrong city.

In the USSR it was completely plausible that you could walk into someone else's apartment in another city and believe it was your own: the odds were that you would probably own the same sofa, the same crockery, the same books, the same TV set. The irony about *The Irony of Fate*, as far as I could see, was that people didn't hate it. Lots of my friends worshipped it. It was their favourite. I had been forced to watch this film at least three times. Now I felt as if I were living in it.

Surely there was something creepy about the fact that certain superficial aspects of your life could be not just *similar* but *exactly the same* whether you lived in Volgograd or Vladivostok – two cities which sound similar to anyone raised in the West, but which are 4000 miles apart, a greater distance than the distance between the east and west coasts of the United States? Was it creepy, though? Or was it reassuring? As an outsider from *tam*, I would never fully understand.

Krivoy Rog means 'Crooked Horn', and the city's strange name has two potential sources. The first is from a village founded in the area, which was built by a one-eyed Cossack ('one-eyed' is the same old word as 'crooked' in Ukrainian) whose name was Rih ('Horn') – so it means 'One-Eyed Cossack by the name of Horn'. A great name for a city. The second – more plausible but less exciting – theory relates to the shape of the two rivers that meet here: the Saksahan and the Inhulets. Their meeting point forms the shape of a crooked horn. Whichever derivation is correct, I was obsessed with this name, and the boys in the band gloried in its weirdness. We all loved that it sounded like a place out of a cowboy movie.

As a city, though, I discovered that it lacked the romanticism that its name suggested. Through the Soviet era, Krivoy Rog was known for being dry and dusty. Across the apartment blocks, people did not string their washing out across balconies and windows in the way they did in St Petersburg in the spring and summer months. In the 1990s, there was so much air pollution that no one even dried their clothes on the balcony because they would become covered in a grey, powdery film. You also felt it in the air: a powdery grittiness that made my nose wrinkle and my eyes itch, leaving me hunting for my rapidly dwindling inhaler.

* * *

I cried when Bogdan's mother opened the door to us, and so did she. She was like so many women in her Soviet generation: ground down by life, old before her time but with a sort of sparkly inner beauty. This impression was enhanced by a full set of gold teeth. There was an immediate warmth between the two of us, and I could sense that she was relieved: whatever the worst-case scenario she might have been expecting, I was not it.

Bogdan's father held back: he had the same kind of shyness as his son, keeping the same kind of respectful distance as Bogdan usually did. We nodded cautiously at each other. It turned out that his father was as tall as his mother was short, which is how Bogdan had ended up in the middle, slightly taller than me. His father was obviously also called Bogdan, but did not have the distinction of having a father called Gift of God. His name was Bogdan Petrovich: Gift of God, son of Peter. Not quite the same effect. But still impressive.

He looked me up and down approvingly, and announced loudly that he would not be putting trousers on for my visit – by which he meant that he hoped no one was offended that he was wearing shorts over his exceptionally long legs. If Misha had been there, I could have made a joke about beautiful legs. But Misha was not there, so I kept my mouth shut. Gift of God Senior wore stripey pool slides on his long, thin feet. He was a handsome, well-preserved man with a tanned face and elegantly cropped silver hair. This was a difference from all my Russian friends: people here were tanned. 'Dad, please. Go and do something on the balcony.' Bogdan Junior was embarrassed. I managed to figure out how to say, 'It's hot. I would also be wearing shorts if I had any.' I was very pleased with myself that I thought to say this.

The atmosphere lightened. 'And another thing,' Bogdan Senior boomed, now emboldened. 'Do not be alarmed but you will see the complete works of Lenin in the toilet. It's ideal for wiping your arse.' He laughed to himself. I pretended not to understand the word 'arse' as it was the sort of word that young ladies were not supposed to use, and had prompted the man who kerb-crawled me to roll up his window and drive off in disgust. I was pretty sure I had heard this joke in many other people's flats before, and I considered telling the Bill Clinton joke in return, but then thought better of it. I was not a man, after all. Better to say less. His father eyeballed me again. *A Tarasa Shevchenko, vana chitala? Has she read Taras Shevchenko?* I had no idea who this was. *Spokino, Tato*, Bogdan shushed him. *Leave it, Dad.*

* * *

When we were alone, I asked who Taras Shevchenko was. Only Ukraine's answer to Shakespeare, apparently. I felt bad. I had never heard of him. Bogdan exhaled. 'Don't worry about it. No one cares about Taras Shevchenko.' We settled in. Bogdan and I would be sharing the sofa bed in the sitting room. But he instructed me not to mention anything about the sleeping arrangements in front of his mother as she had got upset about it. She kept saying, *U nas skrominko . . . We have a humble apartment. . . .* Bogdan's parents' flat was much bigger than the flats I was used to in St Petersburg, but still, it was modest: one bedroom, a sitting room, a kitchen, a tiny bathroom and a separate toilet. The sitting room had a wide balcony that looked out into the gardens. We were high up, on something like the eleventh floor. Birch trees crowded the yard, and the air was soft and warm. There were drab beige tower blocks as far as the eye could see. But the sun baked everything, and the air of neglect and decay that I was used to in St Petersburg was not so obvious. Maybe it was me, all loved-up and romanticising everything . . . *which I knew I was doing even as I was doing it and still couldn't stop myself* . . . or maybe it was the climate – but this place felt more optimistic. It was closer to the sun.

I ignored anything that contradicted this feeling. The same stench of *papyrosy* and *smerdit'* – old man's cigarettes and old man's piss – in the lift. The same metallic tang that pervaded everything in buildings and on public transport, as if all the Soviet metalwork – radiators, lift doors, pipes, handles – had all been made in the exact same factory to the same specifications from the same source materials. It was the smell of *sovok* that followed you everywhere. *Sovok* got into your nostrils and your clothes and your heart and your brain and made you nostalgic for things that were, basically, not particularly nice, but were familiar and predictable. People often spoke of *do vsego etogo, before all this* as if it were a gentler, more innocent time. *Drugoye vremya, another time.* I hadn't even known that time. But I had heard enough of the way people talked about the 1970s and the 1980s to feel as if I knew that time and why the memory of it was somehow precious to people, despite the decay, despite the mess, despite everything.

The words were different here, though, and the way people talked. When I first met the boys from the band, I had not heard Ukrainian accents before, or really, any accents at all. I knew that people from St Petersburg and Moscow could tell each other apart because of their accents. I knew that Gorbachev was from the south of Russia, and was supposed to speak with a pronounced southern accent. With the Ukrainians, I could immediately hear the difference in the way they spoke: they pronounced 'g' as 'h'. So Bogdan pronounced his own name 'Bohdan'. (In Ukrainian, the letter 'g' is pronounced similar to the way we pronounce an aspirated hard 'h' in English.) They said *nie* instead of *nyet* (no), *tak* instead of *da* (yes), *nema* instead of *netu* (there aren't any). Now I had come to a place where everyone talked like this and I could suddenly understand what Bogdan's mother said to me when she said *vin khodiv i khodiv – he walked and walked.*

Lyuba spent most of her time in the kitchen, like many of the mothers I knew during that year. They rarely prepared food in any kind of elaborate way because there wasn't really any food to prepare. Instead they preserved vegetables and fruit for the winter. Or made things with flour. Or they fried things: *blini* (pancakes), *oladiye* (kefir pancakes), *syrniki* (cottage cheese pancakes), bread, cheese, a precious egg, of course . . . but they were generally tidying things, fussing around, making tea, cleaning jars that would be used for pickling, scooping vegetable peelings into newspaper pages, washing up, keeping busy. When you lived and worked in a small space, you had to stay busy keeping it clean and tidy.

She spoke a mix of languages to me, or so it seemed. I don't know now if she was actually speaking *surzhyk* (the 'with rye' language), or if she was speaking Ukrainian but adding in Russian words to help me understand her. Or indeed, if she was just speaking how she always spoke. Either way, we understood each other. On the second day, she gave me a beautiful pair of earrings – ornate filigree with blue stones. I put them on immediately and didn't take them off for weeks. If our conversation was limited sometimes, it was not because of language but because of different horizons. She never asked me a single question about my life back home, about what I thought of Russia or St Petersburg. Things were much simpler. Did

I prefer white bread or black bread? Strawberries or raspberries? Was my hair natural or had I put henna in it? (She put henna in her hair.) I couldn't ask what I wanted to ask even though I knew the words in Ukrainian: *Ya persha divchina? Am I the first girlfriend?*

I made a mistake one day when I was talking to her: I said it was a shame that Bogdan had dropped his studies. I didn't see why he couldn't go to university and be in a band at the same time. It wasn't as if the band was earning him any money anyway. Nor was it like they really had many gigs. There was still no evidence of this 'tour' that we were supposed to be going on. Every day I would ask and every day I would be told, 'We will know soon.'

I knew as soon as I had said the word 'university' to her that my words had been a mistake. It took me by surprise. I wasn't being entirely serious. I was just making conversation. But I had blundered into an area of sensitivity. Lyuba started crying, so much that she couldn't speak. 'I wanted him to study,' she sobbed. 'I wanted him to finish university . . . it's all such a waste. I don't know what will become of him.' She wiped her eyes with an orange flowery tea towel that matched her bright hair, pulled her apron tighter around herself and sniffed hard. She looked at me and patted my head: 'Things are not the same for us as they are for you.' There was a tightness to her mouth that I hadn't seen before. She was right. It was not the same. We sat in silence for a while. After a while she said sadly, 'You will go back There. *Tam.* And you will forget about him.'

It was not a warning or an accusation or a plea. For her it was just a fact. *Tam* was always hanging in the air when I was around. I so wanted her to be wrong. That was not who I was. I didn't care about *tam* any more.

143

The next day, she and I kept our distance from each other. I had hit a nerve and spoken out of turn. Bogdan and I sat in the sitting room, him playing guitar and me singing. Bogdan would always wind me up by playing 'Michelle' by The Beatles, which I found cringey. But sometimes I would humour him by singing the words: he never sang. There was only one Beatles song I loved, which was 'Here, There and Everywhere'. We played it over and over until he had got all the chords right and I had remembered all the lyrics I was ever going to remember – which was not very many of them. 'Again. Start again. Go again,' I would say when I ran out of words. He would pretend to be annoyed, but go straight back to the beginning, as though we were rehearsing for something. We got through the longest version yet before I noticed that his mum had opened the sitting-room door and was standing halfway in, halfway out, crying happy tears.

*   *   *

In Krivoy Rog I couldn't pass for local in the way that I could in St Petersburg. But I couldn't be a tourist either: there wasn't even any Intourist here. My status was uncertain. I told myself that in some ways my relationship with Bogdan couldn't be going better, and finally we were together. But now that I was actually here . . . I was back in another situation where I was beholden to Bogdan and his family, where I needed them to look after me, where I had no independence. Although the summer I had waited for and longed for now stretched ahead, I could suddenly see *the end of the summer* and the fact that I was supposed to start back at university in October. I would need to go home in September. I kept thinking about a girl I had heard of, a few years above me, who had dropped out and got married to her Russian boyfriend. Was that what this was turning into? I still hadn't booked my flight.

In any case, I was about to get a reminder that maybe I was still a child. During the first week at Bogdan's parents, I was brushing my hair in the bathroom. As I looked in the mirror and down at the hairbrush, I froze. I had headlice. There are simply no words to describe the degree of my mortification in that moment. It goes without saying that this was a period in my life when I wanted to appear at the height of attractiveness at all times, and really did not want an insect infestation in my very long and extremely thick hair to add to my insecurities. I had seen a small creature actually crawling in my hair, which I knew meant it was pretty bad, because by the time you can see them and not just feel them, you are beyond the early stages. It meant that probably I had had them before I went on the train journey, before I stayed at Roza's, before. . . well, who could say how long I'd had them? I don't remember my hair being itchy before this happened. But it was hot, and maybe I just hadn't noticed that I'd been scratching. I shuddered.

What was I going to say? Did I know the word for 'headlouse'? I did not. I knew the word for 'bedbug' (*klop*) because it was the title of a play written by Mayakovsky in the late 1920s. But that word was not useful at this moment. I felt physically sick. I had just shared a bed and a pillow with Bogdan. We both had long hair. I had almost certainly given him headlice. (It did not occur to me at this point that it was entirely possible that he had given them to me in the first place.) I tied my hair up in a bun as tightly as possible and headed to the small Russian-English Oxford dictionary I kept at the bottom of my rucksack. The word was there: *vosh, louse, vshi, lice.* I decided I couldn't say it out loud.

I walked over to the balcony where Bogdan was playing the guitar, handed the dictionary to him, pointed to the word and pointed to my head. He couldn't stop laughing.

'But I have probably given them to *you*,' I protested. 'It's not funny. I'm so ashamed. Stop laughing.'

'*Chuchelo, you dummy.*'

'I am not a dummy. *Ya ne chuchelo.*'

'Yes, you are. It's not a big deal. *Kitsia, little kitten.* We will sort this out.'

He still couldn't stop laughing. 'We are going to have to tell your mum,' I said crossly, 'Will she know what to do? Can we go to a chemist or something? I need. . . *lekarstvo*, medicine.' I did not know how to say 'a treatment shampoo for headlice'. Now he thought it was even funnier. *Lekarstvo* is the sort of medicine you drink from a bottle. I was basically saying I needed cough syrup for my headlice.

Still laughing, he took the dictionary into the kitchen and showed it to his mother. She was disbelieving and immediately sat me down and started going through my hair. Eventually she started tutting: *tak, tak, tak, yes, yes, yes*, I had them all right. 'This is the train,' she said solemnly. 'Those trains are disgusting. That's *sovok* for you. They do not clean the linen properly. This is why I will never travel by train. You poor girl.' I was forlorn and whimpered, 'Bogdan, can you ask her about the cough syrup?' She was already sorting through the cupboard underneath the sink. She emerged triumphant with a giant bar of orangey pink soap. It looked like a radioactive version of Pears soap and did not seem convincing as an anti-lice treatment. *Shcho tse What is it?* I asked. *Karbolove milo. Carbolic soap.* I realised that although I could understand the words, I did not actually know what it was. But if *karbolove milo* was all they had, *karbolove milo*

146

would have to do. She looked at me sternly: 'We will all have to wash our hair with it. Several times. Go and take a shower.'

We all spent the morning going in and out of the shower, lathering up our hair. Bogdan Senior was excused from this; being slightly balding, he was considered low-risk.

I was still mortified, but somehow relieved: I had come out the other side of something horrible and survived it. Bogdan did not seem to think I was hideous. He just thought it was funny. And the treatment seemed medieval enough to be effective. After three rounds of furious scalp-scrubbing, Lyuba chased us out of the house to let our hair dry in the sun.

I shudder when I remember all this. But I also marvel at the kindness. Who was I to these people? I wasn't their responsibility. But they took me in and looked after me and treated my lice without a second thought. I did feel grateful. But it was also the moment that I started to think about home – my real home – and my real mum, who prided herself on a well-stocked medicine cabinet and would never have come at me with a bar of *karbolove milo*.

Days came and went in a blur with further anti-lice latherings, much force-feeding of *syrniki* pancakes, regular doses of homemade *mors* (a cranberry drink) and visits to the market for dairy products where I would pretend not to be shocked that these were stocked next to actual giant skinned cow's heads, bloodied and veiny with their eyes protruding and flies buzzing around. We sat on the balcony a lot, and I tried to remember the lyrics of songs that Bogdan could play which were not by The Beatles.

On the days we didn't stay at home, we would go to the band's recording studio, which was not exactly state-of-the-art but was still, amazingly, an actual recording studio. Borys and Artem argued constantly. By this point, the band was onto their third drummer since I had met them. They made angry phone calls to people and counted out small piles of money in roubles and dollars. Various shady local characters came and went. Bogdan and I ignored them, and sat gazing at each other.

The four of them did rehearse, and they put me to work translating and helping them to make sense of song ideas they had. The band's lyrics were ostensibly in English, but they often made little sense to a native English speaker. I thought for a while that this was my fault, that this was a kind of punk poetry that I didn't understand. I had studied Shakespeare briefly at school and was aware that there are certain forms of expression whose meaning and beauty do not present themselves to you immediately. You have to do a bit of work. So I assumed that there must be meaning buried inside the lyrics, and it was up to me to concentrate hard enough to extract it. But no matter how long you frowned over them or suggested alternative phrasings, they just made no sense. This was not surprising as (a) no one in their circle had any command of spoken English and (b) the lyrics had never been exposed to a native English speaker before. Sample lyric: 'I've got bell-bottomed trousers/I walk through pimply mouthers/They look at me, they talk about me/they suck their stinking crosiers.'

I eventually realised an important point. When the lyrics had been written – over the course of long, possibly drink-laced studio sessions with the help of an ancient Soviet Russian-English dictionary – there had never been any suggestion that these 'songs' (they were really shouted 'raps') were likely to reach the ears of anyone who actually spoke English as their mother tongue. So this was a kind of nonsense English written for an audience who did not understand English. According to these criteria, they were extremely successful lyrics.

But now that I had come on the scene, the criteria for the lyrics' success had changed. Suddenly it was imperative that I understood these lyrics, appreciated them, savoured them. I was coming under increasing pressure to translate the lyrics back into Russian in such a way that they made sense; that showed they were profound, even. It was like translating something written by a cat. 'When you say, "They suck their stinking crosiers". . . what exactly do you mean?' There was much miming of the word 'stink' using the international language of nose-pinching. I never really got to the bottom of what they thought a crosier was. I had no idea myself. But maybe that's rock 'n' roll. And I just wasn't cool enough to understand it. Eventually I gave up and signed off the lyrics as perfect. 'Well, it seems to me like you have said what you wanted to say.' I shrugged. *Molodtsi. Well done.*

Every day, I waited for news of the band's big summer tour. Names of different towns flew around: Nikolayev, Dnipropetrovsk, Zaporizhia – and didn't they once say Kiev? I wanted to see Kiev properly. But despite my questions, a tour schedule somehow never materialised. They eventually did book three gigs, all of them in the town of Odessa. At least one of these was a big summer festival.

It turned out that the truth about being invited to 'go on tour' with the band was that they weren't really planning to go anywhere. Still, in the traditional Soviet manner of naming things in such a way that it didn't matter whether they actually existed or not, they somehow thought that, although they were at home and the only travelling they did was to the recording studio or the cigarette kiosk and back, that they were 'on tour.' It eventually dawned on me that there was only one of us actually on tour: me. It was a solo tour: one girl accompanied by a group of guys who wanted mostly to smoke, talk rubbish and crack open sunflower seeds with their teeth.

In the week it took me to realise that there really was no tour, I was constantly told, 'Why do you ask so many questions? Don't be so impatient.' *Shcho bude, to bude. What will be will be.* I couldn't seem to get it into my yoghurt head. It was the one great 'quality' of Soviet life, I suppose: you had no choice but to live in the moment. It was the one habit that had not rubbed off on me. The past was not something anyone wanted to think about, and the future was unknown. There was no point imagining it. *Shcho bude, to bude.*

* * *

The big Odessa festival date was getting closer, and even if the tour only had one stop, we were all excited about it. In the last few days in Krivoy Rog, I visited with Bogdan's granny who told me that I had an arse *yak u vorobya, like a sparrow*, and attempted to fatten me up with fried bread and plums. I could have spent more time with this excellent woman. But finally word had come from the 'sponsors' and the festival organisers that it was time to hit the road. Bogdan's mother was very happy I was going along because 'they will not be so stupid if you are there.' She had no idea. Nothing I had observed about their behaviour over the previous year suggested that me being there would make anyone behave sensibly. They usually got extremely drunk and went to bed at four in the morning. But I was glad she wouldn't be worrying.

We set out on buses with all their equipment in tow. The train was too expensive. Krivoy Rog to Odessa is about six hours by road and we stopped in a few places: Bashtanka, Nikolayev, Yuzhne.

I understood that new gigs were promised if this gig went well, and if the right person was around at the right time, and saw them on stage, and liked them. This sounded like quite a lot of variables to me, but I kept my mouth shut. At last, we were checking into an actual hotel, next to Arkadia Beach in Odessa. My questions here were, as usual, superfluous and resented. I was annoying to everyone at moments like this, asking, 'How long will we be staying here?'

Nikhto ne znaye. No one knows.

'Really? One night or a week?'

Nikhto ne znaye.

'Is breakfast included?'

In response I would get a withering look and a gesture towards the rucksack containing the tins of *tushonka* and peas. I winced.

Tushonka was one of the worst things about staying with the band. They ate – almost exclusively – canned food, mostly vegetables like peas and artichokes, and *tushonka*, a kind of stewed meat. At breakfast they would hack open these cans using a pen knife with no regard for health, safety or hygiene, and then hand them round. If no one had a fork or spoon, they would eat the contents off the back of the pen knife. They were always offended when I didn't want any. *Obidno.*

Even though I felt bad about it because it made me feel snobby and Western, I had a real problem with *tushonka*. This was a Soviet staple, maybe even a delicacy to some; Borys claimed it was his favourite food. It was used as military rations and even as tourist food supplies. Imagine getting that on your traveller's picnic. It looked like corned beef crossed with dog food, and it always had a thick layer of yellowy-white fat on the top which got enthusiastically mixed in with the stringy meat because the fat was 'the best bit'. It was when the *tushonka* came out that I embraced my full inner yoghurt, and claimed I had a headache and wasn't hungry.

I was annoyed with myself in these moments – even though I knew that if any of my British friends were there, they would also find an excuse not to eat the dog food, and they would want to know what time lunch was, and what time the sound check was at the gig. But why couldn't I let things be? Just be in the moment, and not care about what was happening tomorrow, and who was going to be there, and where we would have breakfast? This was one of the biggest differences in our mentalities: the attention devoted to time and money, or to practical organisation in general. I don't think of myself – didn't then, don't now – as a person who is particularly materialistic or capitalist, or even someone who is especially organised. But at these kinds of moments, I was always reminded of the fact that I had grown up with ideas like 'Time is money', and 'Money doesn't grow on trees', and 'There's no such thing as a free lunch.' I could never get my head around the elasticity of time that seemed so natural to the band. 'Who cares what day it is? You ask too many questions. It's a Western habit. Let it go. Relax. Let things be.' As Misha liked to say: *Polny relax.*

Amazingly, Bogdan and I had our own room, the biggest room 'for the foreigner'. But having the biggest room also meant that everyone else came and lived in it, smoked in it, used our shower, and came in to ask me last-minute follow-up questions about crosiers. I was not going to be hanging out in that room if I could avoid it. The rest of the hotel was ugly and hostile: a cross between a venue for a Politburo party conference and something out of *The Shining.* But none of this mattered because the city of Odessa itself was incredible. It looked like Venice or Paris: wide streets with

French and Italian 19th-century architecture. This was a more decadent, Italianate take on the type of post-Soviet seaside experience I
had only seen before in Latvia. Odessa was on a different scale, and
it was glorious: beaches where people were sunbathing, swimming
and eating *voblya* (dried fish); kiosks serving sangria, Eskimo Soviet
choc ices and decadent Western Snickers ice cream. If I had known
about this place, this is where I would have spent the whole year. It
was less stressful than St Petersburg: elegant, charming, welcoming.
I also felt safe walking here on my own – maybe because it was
warm, and people lived outdoors, so the streets were always busy.
Or maybe because it somehow felt as if it had escaped the grip of
sovok, as if it had kept something of its own character.

I got away from them all in the mornings, and walked the streets
feeling free and happy. No one followed me. No one asked me to
change money. I didn't have to be ready to tell someone the time at
a moment's notice. And in the evenings, there was something about
the light of the late summer nights that was romantic and beautiful
and just made you want to burst out laughing. Bogdan and I sat on
the beach and watched the sunset. We visited dozens of kiosks in
order to ascertain which one served the cheapest kebabs, which I
would occasionally be permitted to buy if I was alone with Bogdan.
He loved what he called *shaverma*, a grilled meat wrap, and it was
one of the only things he would let me treat him to. He didn't want
me to have to pay for everyone, partly because it was embarrassing
and partly because they could eat a lot of kebabs. We argued about
whether I was spending too much money on Snickers ice cream,
which cost about 20 times the price of local ice cream. And we
argued about whether it was worth spending money on souvenirs
at the Potemkin Steps, the extraordinary 142-metre stone staircase

that features in Eisenstein's 1925 film *Battleship Potemkin*. It stretches down to the harbour and is designed in such a way that it appears much longer and much wider than it really is.

By the time we made it to the summer festival, I was on a high. This was it, the moment that the whole summer had been building up to. Finally they had a gig on the scale Kuznetsov had been promising for months but never quite delivered. The band was finally going to get their chance. This was the big time.

* * *

The festival was in some kind of open space, an amphitheatre in a big park. We had gone early so that they could scope out the performance area. The festival seemed well organised: lights, sound check, technicians. The stage was huge, unlike anywhere I had seen them perform before. During the sound check, Bogdan was way over one side of the stage and could barely see Borys on bass on the other side. They had done a short tune-up before anyone really arrived, and then we went to hang out in the green room. On stage, there were lots of roadies, state-of-the-art equipment, massive sound systems; backstage, though, was weirdly low-key. Something about the atmosphere immediately seemed off to me, but I was so used to things seeming bizarre, only to be told that they were totally normal, that I just ignored this feeling. *Davai pokurim. Let's have a cigarette.*

In the green room, I tried to look more excited than I was. It was a hot day and they had cold Borjomi in the fridge. I had never seen any of them drink water before. They were taking this gig seriously. We sat around and waited, everyone smoking endlessly as usual. I thought about the week Bogdan and I had had in Odessa. In some ways, the whole summer I'd been waiting for had happened in that one week. The last few nights had been magical, despite the constant threat of canned meat. My solitary mornings had given me a daily moment to myself. At lunchtimes, the guys would surface and play their guitars for a bit, then we would head to the party house where there seemed to be a short-lived supply of gorgeous *saperavi* (Georgian red wine), an endless stream of horrible *portvein* (fortified red wine), beer, vodka and cartons of random sticky tropical juices. Odessa was full of artists, musicians and hangers-on, and every night was *tusovka* (the party zone). Borys knew someone who knew someone with a ramshackle villa in the heart of town with dozens of rooms and a patio garden with a grapevine pergola.

Sure, this was *romantichny* – there was a romance to all this. And I would sit on the beach with my chin cupped in my hand, looking out on the Black Sea, mooning and sighing over Bogdan and how handsome he was, in the same way I had done all year since that night in Kosmos. But there was an undertow creeping in. I was drinking a lot of beer and smoking a lot of cigarettes, which wasn't healthy. And I was like a nun compared to Bogdan and the guys. They even drank extremely nasty *konyak* at breakfast, which was more like a sort of alcoholic molasses. Bogdan was particularly bad, and we had started to bicker about his drinking. I felt as if he was avoiding something. He wasn't entirely avoiding *me*, though. He wanted me to be alone and sit with him while he was drinking. If I questioned him too hard or brought him a soft drink, he would stare at me and crack up as he intoned, *Bukhat'!* This meant he was on a mission. *Bukhat'* means to drink with the express purpose of getting completely off your face. There had been times at these events when I would fall asleep as people were partying around me, and eventually he would fall asleep too. We woke up one morning in the party villa still in our clothes, hot and sunburnt, the sun streaming through the grapes. It was so hot I felt as if the grapes had dripped onto me, but I was just sweating from Obolon – the non-alcoholic-beer-that-was-actually-alcoholic – and from self-loathing.

I guess I thought the festival experience would make everything right and set me and Bogdan back on track: it would have all been worth it. Instead it was all slipping away. I suddenly realised what was wrong backstage. There was no one else around. No managers, no talent scouts, no A&R people, no hangers-on, not even any other groupies for me to be jealous of. This was not how it was supposed to be. There was supposed to be noise and glamour and excitement and the buzz of a big crowd and that feeling that, yes, finally, they've arrived. I suddenly felt very protective of the Colney Hatch boys. This was their big day. This was the moment we had all waited for. I looked around and thought: *Ya odna. I am alone.* And worse than that: *What if I am their only fan?* They headed to the stage, Bogdan and Borys with their guitars slung over their shoulders like they always wore them, Artem ruffling his hair and rolling his shoulders, warming up. They were striding and full of purpose, headed for glory. They took their positions on stage and Borys struck a low bass chord. It was late afternoon and the sun was blazing. From the wings, I could see Bogdan squint as he glanced out into the crowd. *Khallo Odessa!* Artem screamed into the mic.

With the sound technicians and the flash lighting rig, this performance had all the hallmarks of the cinematic Fleetwood Mac 'summer of love' vibes I had envisaged. They had this giant stage to themselves, they had their rocking long hair and their red guitars. But I caught the doubletake on Bogdan's face as he looked out into the audience.

Where was everyone? Shcho tse? What's going on? We had arrived at lunchtime and had been hanging out in the green room for a couple of hours. I had assumed the park would fill up by late afternoon and they'd be looking out on a sea of faces grooving to the beat like something out of Woodstock. Sure, there were some people there – maybe several hundred. The lyrics I had tried and failed to translate blared out across the park. 'I'm not drunk/It's only fucking funk.' It was a gigantic space, and the people were spread out. Worse, they were paying no attention to what was happening on stage. 'I've got bell-bottomed trousers/I walk through pimply mouthers.' This was not a rock concert vibe. There were families having picnics. 'They suck their stinking crosiers.' Groups of teenage girls sat in a circle sunbathing and oblivious to the music. Colney Hatch might as well have been busking outside the metro. It was a massive anti-climax. And I knew that we would never speak of it again.

I danced to their terrible songs in the wings and tried to look as enthusiastic as possible, giving it the full Stevie Nicks. Seeing as no one else there appeared to have any enthusiasm for them, I owed them it. I guess at least I had got what I wanted. If anyone had taken a photo of me in that moment, I would have looked like the perfect rock chick: 21 years old, long hair swinging, cute mini-dress, knee-high boots despite the heat, soaking up the sunlight bouncing off the stage lights. Out of all their gigs, it was almost certainly the worst. But it was maybe the one I loved the best.

* * *

After the non-event of the festival the mood was sombre. I thought about making some elaborate statement about my views on the post-Soviet world and how nothing was ever quite as it seemed, but that was the whole joy of *sovok*, right? Misha would have appreciated this sentiment. But it didn't need to be said out loud. And we were all intensely focused on pretending that everything had gone as expected. Except for Borys, who was intensely focused on the dwindling number of cans of boiled meat. The trip back from Odessa to Krivoy Rog involved some kind of a stopover in Nikolayev, a shipbuilding centre, to drop off a package or call in on some unexplained person or run some errand that no one could quite explain to me. I remember only vague things about this place, like the amusing sci-fi-sounding word Nibulon (a shipyard) and the Yantar (amber) Brewery. There must have been a lot of beautiful buildings that we could have visited. We stayed in some kind of *spalny rayon* and there, once again, were what seemed like miles and miles of the type of apartment blocks depicted in *The Irony of Fate*.

As usual, I wanted to know why we were stopping here and when we were leaving and all sorts of other pointless yoghurt questions. What were we 'dropping off'? But there was nothing weird or illegal or nefarious going on, I eventually realised. It was just another reminder that people didn't think things through in the way that I had been raised to, and after all this time, I still didn't get it. Our concept of 'trust' was completely different. If I needed to send a package to a relative in another part of the UK, I would entrust it to the Royal Mail. Here, you delivered parcels by hand if remotely possible, even if it was out of your way, and even if it meant we all had to stay in a random apartment with more new random unknown people.

There was nothing unsafe about any of this, intrinsically. But I was beginning to feel more and more adrift. These people went with the flow. They accepted hospitality when it was offered. They didn't worry about what was coming tomorrow, or work to any particular plan. They didn't ask specific questions about what a festival would be like and how many tickets had been sold. They said yes to things if they felt like it, and then didn't turn up if they didn't feel like it. There was not much point in planning anything when the money you had in your pocket would be worth tomorrow half what it was worth today. It was futile to try to go about things in an organised and logical way when all around you people were giving and taking bribes, fiddling the system, getting from day to day. I guess they had lived like this for a while, and it had become habit. I had tried and failed to get to the same state.

Bogdan started saying *bukhat'* to me more and more often. I was kind of starting to miss Misha. Sure, Misha drank too, but he would never speak to me like that, and you could have a proper conversation with him. He was really the only beacon of sanity amongst all the friends I had made over the past year. He was the only one I could really talk to, and there were so many things that I wanted to run past him. Had I been stupid to think there would be an actual tour, with well-attended gigs and some semblance of a schedule, and that we would have an amazing time? Why did Bogdan seem indifferent towards me some of the time? And was it OK for the boys in the band to be drinking as much as they were drinking? Was it normal? And if it wasn't normal . . . what, then?

When we left Odessa, we had packed in a hurry, hungover. As I went through my bag over and over in Nikolayev, I realised I couldn't find my favourite dress. It was a cute summer dress I had bought on a hot, sweltering day in Paris in the weeks before I left for St Petersburg. I found it in a shop near the Gare du Nord. I had very few clothes that had lasted the year and I loved that dress. It was all too much. I started crying hysterically, pulling all of Bogdan's stuff out of his bag in case he had it. He didn't. I was sobbing and hiccupping too much to explain what was wrong. *Vivka, shcho? Shcho s toboyu? What, Vivka, what's with you?* Of course, I was not really crying about the dress, but about the frustration and the strangeness and the occasional wondrousness of that whole summer and what had to happen next . . . because I knew then that all of this was going to have to come to an end. And this was the sign: a summer dress which probably didn't fit me anyway because I had eaten too many Snickers ice creams. *Vazhlivoye vtracheno, poteryano.* I was babbling, mixing up Russian and Ukrainian words, like the 'with rye' language. *Something special and I've lost it.*

I wanted it back. I insisted to Bogdan that we call the hotel from *The Shining* and ask them to find the dress. He was surprisingly amenable to this. Or possibly he just did not want to argue with me when I was hysterical. *Davai, chuchelo. Come on, you idiot scarecrow. We'll find a phone.* We sourced as many *dvushki* coins as we could for the phone booth. In Ukraine at that time, you were very lucky if you could find a payphone that worked. And you were even luckier if you had one of the rare two-kopek coins that you needed for the phone – a *dvushka* or twopenny piece. I realised that Bogdan must have used up loads of *dvushki* when he was trying to track me down at Roza's. The *dvushka* was going out of circulation so people actually paid more money for one than it was worth. Imagine that back in the day, payphones could only be operated using a ten-pence coin. But ten-pence coins are hard to come by, so when you get one, you charge people a pound to have it. This was the life of the *dvushka*. People tried other things: using buttons, jamming a knife in the phone slot, using foreign coins. But the *dvushka* was not easily imitated.

Still, we found some. How did we find the hotel's phone number? This was at a time when people still called the operator to get connected to a number. Or someone must have had a business card or a bill from the hotel. In any case, we got through to someone, and I started to explain into the weird antiquated Soviet phone booth receiver down a crackly line what had happened and that this dress was very precious. 'It's somewhere in our room. . . maybe under the sink. Please find it. I bought it in Paris.' I started to get nervous that if I made out that the dress was too special, someone might think it was valuable and want to steal it. This made me start crying again.

Bogdan was getting annoyed now. 'Why are you telling them about Paris? They will want a bribe.' *Dai trubku. Give me the phone.* He grabbed the receiver and took charge, explaining that he was a student from Krivoy Rog, which amused me, because it would have made his mother very happy to hear him say this, but he was only saying it to imply that we were ordinary people and not the sort of people who bought dresses in Paris. I heard him explain that it was not so much a dress as I had described it but a *sarafan*. I thought this word meant 'scarf' or 'shawl'. I looked at him daggers. It was not a scarf. *Kakoi tebe sarafan?* I hissed accusingly. *What are you on about, a* scarf? I shouted *Eto platye – it is a dress!* – into the phone receiver. *Eto sarafanchik*, he continued, using the affectionate diminutive. *It is a tiny little scarf*, I suppose he was trying to say. 'It's a wisp of a dress. It's easily missed. Please check your lost property and the bin.' Which was kind of him. And to be fair it was kind of a throwaway summer dress. But still! My lovely dress was not a *sarafan* or a scrap of fabric. So irritating. I couldn't shake the tantrum. He, however, could still be sweet with me, even when I was unbearable. *Kitsia, come on. Kitten, let's go to the kiosk and get you a teeny tiny little chocolate bar. Plakat' ne nado. It is not necessary to cry.*

I found out later, much later, that I was totally wrong that day. *Sarafan does* mean *summer dress* in Ukrainian and he was not winding me up. Even in Russian, *sarafan* doesn't mean scarf or shawl, as I insisted it did. It means *traditional peasant's pinafore dress*. But back then, I thought I was right. And I harangued him for the rest of the day with great certainty about how my dress was not a *sarafan* and that now they would never find it as they would be looking for a scarf instead of a dress. Except this wasn't what I was saying. I was effectively screaming at him: *MY DRESS IS NOT A DRESS, IT IS A DRESS*. Things had reached their only logical conclusion: this wasn't just a case of 'lost in translation'. I was now speaking fluent gibberish. Fluent scarecrow, I guess. After months of trying and failing to fit in, and trying to think and act like everyone around me, and trying to reconcile all the times when people told me that something was definitely one thing and I could clearly see that it definitely wasn't, this was perhaps the most Soviet thing I had ever said. Even as I ranted and raved and was so sure that I was right, here was the moment when I understood: I had totally lost my mind. It was also the beginning of the end of our relationship. They never did send me the *sarafan*.

grandmother's summer, adj. n.
бабье лето, bab'e leto (Russian)
бабине літо, babyne lito (Ukrainian)

There is an expression for 'Indian summer' in Ukrainian which is shared by other Slavonic languages: *babine leto*. It means an unseasonably late summer, a warm September, a summer that seems to last into winter. And when I returned to St Petersburg in September 1994, that year people were muttering '*babine leto*' (in Ukrainian) or '*bab'e leto*' (in Russian). There are lots of theories why this time of the year is called 'old lady summer' or 'grandmother's summer'. It has a parallel meaning in Russia, Ukraine, Belorussia (now Belarus), Serbia, Bosnia, Croatia, Poland. One theory is that it means the 'second summer' of a woman's life: it is short-lived, ill-timed and illusory. (I'm saying nothing.) The other explanation is that it derives from the ancient word for woman – 'baba' – which survives across many European and Slavic cultures. Baba is the great goddess. And *babine lito* (a last gasp of summer) is her gift. Whichever way you look at it, returning to this old granny summer, I felt that I had suddenly aged.

I was still barely 21, but had returned to St Petersburg in some ways more grown-up. The summer in Ukraine was over. I wasn't headed 'home' for another few weeks. And yet I wasn't sure I even wanted to go 'home', since I didn't really know where that was any more. My university life – and my family life in England – seemed like another era, another world. I couldn't imagine returning to it. But all the ways in which I had tried to 'belong' over the summer had not really worked either.

The sweetness and gentleness that came so naturally to Bogdan were beginning to irritate me. Where once I thought he was enigmatic and aloof, now I thought he was passive and weak. He was only my boyfriend because I kind of made him be my boyfriend. He put in pretty much no effort and didn't want to engage with anything that bothered me. Two things were worrying me most. One: he wouldn't talk about the future at all. Not even about tomorrow – let alone about next month or next year, or about me going to live in another country. Two: he drank too much. I mean, I also drank too much around this time. But I would only drink to excess if it was normal alcohol. He would drink whatever there was. It made me feel nauseous to see him and the guys throwing back shots of 'cognac' that cost about 40p a bottle or 'vodka' that smelled like petrol. I once emptied a bottle of some *samogon*, moonshine, down the plughole when he tried to drink it at breakfast. He thought I was being ridiculous.

He had travelled back to St Petersburg with me on the train, leaving the other guys in the band behind for once. Without them, something was missing. It was more obvious that we had little to say to each other unless I kept up the conversation. When we got back to the city, taking overnight trains all the way so we wouldn't have to pay to stay in Kiev or Moscow, there was a sense of unease hanging over us. Some nights he stayed at mine. But other nights he stayed at Misha's to hang out with other Ukrainians staying there. I had three weeks left before I was going home. I couldn't understand why he didn't want to be with me.

Things really came to a head once when I went over to Misha's one Sunday. They had all been drinking all day. There were people there I didn't know and everyone was off their faces. Even Misha was tipsy, which was unusual; I had never seen him drunk. The place was a tip, with open cans of food everywhere, cigarette butts, empty water bottles. The only thing that confused me was that I couldn't see any empty alcohol bottles anywhere. 'What have you been drinking?' I raised my eyebrows at the stench of the alcohol which was oozing out of everyone's pores. *Spirt*, Misha said sheep-ishly. 'What is "*spirt*"?' I thought that this must be some kind of brand name like Sprite lemonade. They had been drinking *soft drinks and water*? 'It's alcohol. Pure alcohol,' he replied, 'You dilute it with water to drink it.' I still didn't understand. 'Say the name of it again. Spell it.' '*S-p-i-r-t*.'

The penny dropped. He meant literally pure alcohol or spirit. They had been drinking white spirit. 'Show me.' Misha found a plastic bottle with some 'spirit' swishing around the bottom. I sniffed it. Yeah, I was right. This seemed like the kind of liquid my dad used at home to clean paint brushes. I dry-retched slightly. (I realised later that there is a difference between turpentine, white spirit and surgical spirit. But much like the *sarafan*, this distinction felt academic at the time.) 'Vivka, come here and give me a kiss,'

Bogdan lurched towards me. 'You're joking, right? How are you not ashamed?' 'Oh, don't be like that. You need a drink . . . Zheka, have we got any *portvein*?' Orgasmic noises floated towards us from the bathroom. Random people were having sex in the shower. I glowered at Misha. He was supposed to be above all this.

I felt physically sick. How had I ended up with these people? What was I doing here? What was there to be salvaged from all this? I didn't feel frightened, just depressed and really, really tired. I sat down in one of the Formica chairs by the window overlooking the same grey courtyard and the same 'standard apartments' like the ones in the film, and lit a cigarette. 'Vivka, give us some cigarettes.' 'Take them. Just leave me in peace.' Was I being a party pooper? Or a stuck-up yoghurt? Bogdan was always worrying that things were 'not good enough for you'. Maybe he was right. This wasn't good enough for me. I was being a snob. My immediate thought was that I should have given them money for alcohol to stop them from drinking white spirit. But my second thought was: that is hardly a solution. I needed to get out of there and clear my head. And I needed Bogdan to come with me. I had to convince myself that this was not who he was.

'Bogdanchik. Tiny little Bogdan. I'm going home. I'm taking the metro. *Provazhai menya.*' *Accompany me.* '*Da, Vivka, ne khochetsya.*' *I don't feel like it.* Misha butted in: '*Ya tebya provazhayu.*' *I will accompany you.* Poor Misha. He looked so awkward. Even he had days when things got out of control and *chuvaki* (dudes) overtook his apartment and partied too hard. Bogdan put his coat on: 'All right, all right, I'm coming.' In that moment he was sober enough – and maybe still liked me enough? – that he didn't want Misha to see me out.

We walked in silence to the metro. Bogdan was sheepish and giggling like a child caught eating sweets by his mother. He thought I was annoyed because he was drunk. It was going to be too much for me to explain that I didn't so much mind drunkenness as the depravity represented by drinking white spirit. I knew he would pull me up for double standards on this and, who knows, maybe he was right. Alcohol is alcohol. If you're going to get yourself into a mess, maybe it doesn't really matter where the poison comes from.

He sobered up at the station. I bought him a bottle of Coke and more cigarettes. I figured I would make a fry-up when we got back to the apartment. Maybe we could even have a decent evening together. We were still not really speaking as we took the long, long escalator down into the metro. Misha's place was in the same area as the hostel where I had started the year: Prospekt Proschvisheniya. The Avenue of Education. Well, I suppose this had been an education of sorts.

We got on the train into town and were still silent as we sat through the passing stations. We weren't holding hands or touching. We were both in our separate worlds, me watching the two of us in the window opposite, seeing how he was still beautiful and also, after almost a year, still a complete stranger to me. The stations flashed by, him giggling to himself, me livid. I was suddenly gripped by a huge ball of anger and sadness in the pit of my stomach. What the hell was this? What was I doing with this person? He didn't care about me at all. It had never been real. *Ya odna. I am on my own.* So I might as well be on my own. Without even thinking about it, at the next stop when the doors opened, I stood up and got off the train. He didn't stand up to follow me. He just looked up. 'Vivka?' The doors closed. I stood and watched him pass by in the windows. His face showed a hint of surprise but mostly indifference.

Now I really was on my own, and I didn't quite know what to do. I think I had thought – or hoped – that he would follow me or would at least be more annoyed. That there would be some kind of reaction. I waited for the next train and got on it. I got off at the next stop, thinking and hoping that he would have got off there and waited for me. But no. There was no sign of him. I waited for a while, giving him one last chance, sitting on the bench on the train platform, trying not to cry because that would make me a target for some nosy passer-by who would ask me the time. I sniffed hard and pulled myself together. Several empty trains passed. The station stayed empty. It was a Sunday and there was hardly anyone around. Once four or five trains had passed, I realised that he wasn't coming for me. I took the next train home on my own.

*   *   *

For the rest of that September, despite the white spirit and that metro journey, Bogdan and I still pretended there was something between us. He came back to the apartment later that evening and was contrite. He stayed with me for the rest of the month and saw me off at the airport, with Misha in tow, of course. After the *spirit* incident, Misha was *always* in tow, trying to get back into my good books. It's strange, but I have no memory of saying goodbye to Bogdan when I flew home. I just remember his face on the metro from that day I stepped off the train carriage and the doors closed between us. The face I remember from the moment it was time to fly home was Misha's. He came to see me off, in the heat of that

Indian summer, in one of his ludicrous floor-length 'agent of estate' coats and a moss-coloured trilby. He turned his face as I waved goodbye so I wouldn't see his expression. Was he crying? Or did I just want to think he was crying?

When I got back home to my parents and to university, Bogdan and I were in touch by phone every other week or so. Was there something still there? I didn't know. I was in a mess, wanting to drop out of university and return to Russia. Nothing made sense to me any more, and I didn't want to be whatever version of myself I needed to be in order to live in England. I had been locked into doing things that made no sense for so long that I found myself doing the ludicrous thing I had promised Kuznetsov I would do. I made reel-to-reel tapes of Colney Hatch music, looked up the addresses of record labels in the Yellow Pages, and made phone calls to ask the names of people in the A&R departments. I packaged up the tapes and sent them first class from the post office in my parents' town. No one would have known if I had done this or not. But *I* knew I had done it. It seems superfluous to say that I never heard back from anyone.

Even though I knew that by this point there was nothing left to go back to Russia for, I booked a flight back to St Petersburg for December. At the same time, I booked in with the university counselling service. A nice lady therapist let me cry and bleat on about how disappointing my one Ukrainian summer had been and how pointless my life at home felt and how I couldn't bear to go to the supermarket because there was too much food there. I told her about the time Boris Yeltsin went on a diplomatic trip to America and visited a food store in Texas and realised that communism was a lie. It didn't help that at this point I had just realised that

I still had headlice. 'It all sounds pretty overwhelming,' she said, sympathetically.

Hearing myself voice my anxieties out loud made me realise that I sounded like a spoiled foreigner. It was time to pull myself together and get on with things. It still didn't occur to me that one way of doing that would have been to cancel the flight I'd just booked. For that New Year's visit in December 1994, things got off to a bad start when Bogdan met me from the airport with Misha. I shouldn't have been surprised. But why couldn't Bogdan meet me on his own? Why did everything always have to be done with other people like we all lived in some kind of invisible *kommunalka*? I had done my hair and was dressed up for the flight, wearing Lyuba's earrings. Bogdan took one look at the red skirt I was wearing and said, *Pokhozhe na Ded Moroz. She looks like Father Christmas.* The two of them cracked up. I gave Misha a look. He at least had the grace to look guilty. I was beginning to see how it had been all along. We were just a bunch of kids, hanging out, saying stupid things, smoking and passing the time. That was all it had ever been.

Something had shifted while I was away. Misha was in charge and Bogdan seemed to have grown up ever so slightly. The two of them were living together and things with the band seemed to be on hold. At least this time they were in a decent flat in a decent part of town, near the Smolny Cathedral. The apartment looked as if it hadn't been renovated since the 1917 revolution, but it was big, with several bedrooms. It was an upgrade of sorts. I was just happy to be seeing Bogdan, to work out if we could salvage anything.

Meanwhile the news on the TV at home and when I arrived in St Petersburg was brutal, and it was about a place I knew nothing about: Chechnya. As usual, when some huge world event happened that appeared to be stressful and terrible – it was the beginning of the first Chechen war and the New Year's Eve storming of Grozny – everyone shrugged and told me it was nothing. This included the usually sensible Misha, who I begged to explain to me what was happening. *Nakhren tebe eta Chechnya, Vivka. What the hell is Chechnya to you anyway?* If anything, the more time went by, the more they shut their eyes to whatever was not directly in front of them.

Despite me constantly badgering them to explain Chechnya, the news swiftly faded into the background when Misha and Bogdan's housemate Adam started going on about *chesotka*. This was a word I didn't know and couldn't begin to guess. I asked him to explain it and realised slowly that it was a medical condition, one that caused itching. That much I might have guessed: *chesyat'sya* is *to itch*, so *chesotka* sounds a bit like *the itch*. I thought maybe he was trying to tell me that he had eczema or – God forbid – some kind of sexually transmitted disease. This was *prostoy herpes* all over again. But no. It was worse.

I had lugged a huge dictionary over with me on this visit because I had to finish a university project. I was writing my dissertation on the poet Anna Akhmatova's major work *Poem Without a Hero*. I had decided to write it in Russian and Misha was helping me with some of the phrases in it. I needed the dictionary to help me with words like 'simile' and 'self-expression' and all the other important pretentious things I wanted to include. What I did not expect was that I would be using this dictionary to look up *chesotka* and find the word 'mange'. My usual self-preservation instinct kicked in immediately: total denial. What else was I going to do? Stay somewhere else? Phone my parents? Go home? I unlearned the word and the fact of his condition as soon as Adam had said he had it, shut my eyes tight at night and prayed that (a) Bogdan did not already have mange and (b) that I would not catch mange. My prayer worked. We stumbled through the next few days mange-free, me trying to write my dissertation and work out where Chechnya was, all of us smoking fifty million cigarettes and seeing in the New Year with Crimean sparkling wine and Olivier salad.

For the next six months, I still phoned Bogdan on and off, mostly to check that he had not developed mange. But my heart had gone out of it. His reply to most situations was still in one word: *bukhat'* – let's get drunk. And although there was a fondness between us, and he had turned out to be a sweet person, I knew deep down that it was all over. I just couldn't quite admit it on the surface. I didn't really give up on him until after I graduated, by which time we hadn't seen each other for half a year. Plus, just as he had been a sort of a 'cover' for me all that year in St Petersburg, he was a useful absent accessory to have in the year I was taking my finals. I didn't need to believe that I felt lonely or wanted to go out with someone if I had 'a Ukrainian boyfriend in St Petersburg'. I could just concentrate on my exams. In this sense, Bogdan really had ended up being the perfect boyfriend: God's gift for completely different reasons than originally intended.

That trip in early 1995 would be the last time I would see him for another three years. The last time we ever met – in Moscow in 1998 – was not an attempt to get back together. I was in town for a few days for work. He was working in a warehouse. The band had split up. He had lost touch with Misha. Bogdan had plans to make a life in Moscow – it was the only place you could get work. In some ways it was good to see him and really know – with no regrets – that not only was it all over but probably it had never really existed in the first place. I couldn't see the godlike young man I had met in the nightclub a couple of years before. Not because he had changed much physically – although we both looked older and more tired – but because everything about him was different and everything about me was different. The innocence was gone from both of us. *Os shcho. I guess that's that.*

afterword, n.
послесловие, poslesloviye (Russian)
післямова, pislyamova (Ukrainian)

For several nights after Russia invaded Ukraine in February 2022, I had vivid dreams about that train ride with Roza. The Russian phrase *umom Rossii ne ponyat'* kept swirling around my mind. It was a poetry quote that dated from the summer I met Dima, when I had just started living with Elizaveta Dmitrievna, with her sign language and lone tomato. I was taking intensive language classes that summer in a university building behind the Kazan Cathedral, just over the road from the potato church and the cavernous theatre-warehouse. Our teacher was an extraordinary, ancient woman who had a bun on top of her head which made her look like a human cottage loaf. She dressed like a cross between Miss Marple and Miss Trunchbull in Roald Dahl's *Matilda*: a 19th-century school matron who really loved grey tweed and sturdy brown shoes. She was stern but adorable, and taught her classes as if the Soviet Union had never existed.

This teacher never referenced anything that had happened in the past hundred years, and only taught language and literature that dated back to the era of her favourite poet Fyodor Tyutchev (1803–1873). Every day at the start of class, we would recite these four lines from his most famous poem. It was now, 30 years later, that I started to hear the words of this poem first in my sleep, then in my every waking moment.

Умом Россию не понять,
Аршином общим не измерить:
У ней особенная стать –
В Россию можно только верить.

I didn't really understand this poem when I first learned it by heart. Nor did I have the means to look up who Tyutchev was and whether I should pay much attention to him. But the translation I formulated in my mind reflected what I was already beginning to understand about Russia at the time. This is what it means literally: 'You cannot understand Russia with your mind. Nor measure Russia by any average standard. Russia has a special kind of status. You just have to believe in it.' It is written in a beautiful meter, and it sounds wonderful when spoken in Russian, even if you have no idea what the words mean. It is a poem that says, 'Don't ask too many questions and certainly don't engage your intellect. This is a great country. Just keep the faith.' This always seemed to me to be an expression not of pride nor of greatness but of total madness.

* * *

Sometimes you see history happen over the course of a weekend. Like the political coup that I saw on television with Masha and Dasha – *chrezvychainoe polozheniye*, the *emergency position*. That was over in a few days. And sometimes things happen in such slow motion that you look up one day and find that you are 30 years older and everything has turned out the opposite of how you expected. There are so many obvious truths that only emerge with hindsight, that come with that flash of realisation that something has been staring you in the face all along.

People always say that if you are in a certain place at a certain time then you have a ringside seat to history. But that's just not true. You can be right in the middle of history happening and not be able to make head nor tail of it. I worked on the city newspaper in St Petersburg for six months in 1994 and I don't remember once hearing about a civil servant in his early forties who went by the name of Vladimir Putin. He worked in the mayor's office in St Petersburg, having returned from his KGB posting in Dresden in 1990. That office is round the corner from the place where I was staying for New Year, the flat where we all had to work out if we had mange. Nothing is inevitable. Until you see it in the rear-view mirror, and there it was all along. None of us could have predicted that dusty old Krivoy Rog would produce a president for Ukraine. Volodymyr Zelenskyy was born there in 1978, and would have been a teenager a few years younger than Bogdan when I was there, retching over the bloodied cows' heads at the market, drying my carbolic-soap-smelling hair in the sun and going on the third cigarette kiosk run of the day.

When I was an undergraduate studying the history of the region – or rather, The Region – we were repeatedly asked to write essays about what had caused the fall of the Soviet Union. We would rehearse the usual arguments: the corrupt political system collapsing in on itself, the growth of nationalism in different regions, a dysfunctional economy, Gorbachev's democratic reforms, the impact of Chernobyl, the psychological effect of the fall of the Berlin Wall. . . . But the truth was, in the West we were surprised and flummoxed that this supposedly colossal world power had just kind of given up on itself. Many of my professors struggled to answer this question themselves in the mid 1990s, and were more comfortable talking about what had happened in the 1950s and 1960s.

After 1991, a lot of archives were opened which had previously been inaccessible. All kinds of documents were now available to study. Suddenly there was a glut of information, evidence, new theories on the past 70 years. But even then it was clear that there was only one real answer to the question 'What caused the collapse of the USSR?' and it was this: 'What makes you think the Soviet Union has collapsed?'

I started to lose touch with all the Ukrainians from 1998 onwards, although I still messaged with Misha on and off. Misha was the first person to mention Ukrainian nationalism in a positive and enthusiastic way to me. He was the person who told me, when Putin first emerged, that Putin is not someone you have an opinion about because *Putin – eto fakt. Putin is a fact. Vivka, think about it. There's no point in having opinions about facts.* He sent me books written in Ukrainian and asked me if I could get them reviewed in the British press. We still spoke in Russian with each other, but every email he sent would have more Ukrainian in it than the last one. The last time I saw him was in Kiev in 1999. It was long before people had started saying 'Kyiv'. I visited him and his wife with my British husband.

Misha begged me to start learning Ukrainian properly and to forget about Russian entirely. He raised a toast: *Za Ukrainsku movu! To the Ukrainian language! Vivka, I'm telling you, it's the future.* I thought he was exaggerating. I thought the future had room for everything and no one would need to choose. I thought it would all be OK. *Budu vivchati nehaino*, I replied. *I will learn some immediately. Strictly directly.*

Acknowledgements

Thank you to all the team at PEN International for their support in enabling all author proceeds for this book to go towards their work with writers at risk. Thanks especially to Paul Julien and Romana Cacchioli at PEN International and Daniel Gorman at English PEN for their enthusiasm and advice. For more information on their work, go to www.peninternational.org.

All my thanks to my brilliant agent Cathryn Summerhayes and all the team at Curtis Brown for their cheerleading and expertise. All agent fees in association with this book are also being donated to PEN International. Thanks so much to Curtis Brown for facilitating that. To Cathryn and to Jess Molloy, Annabel White and Katie McGowan, I really appreciate what you do for me day in, day out – and especially in regard to this book.

Thanks so much to Sarah Braybrooke, who saw the potential in this book from the beginning and was instrumental in bringing it to life. To all the editing, PR, marketing, audio and design team at Bonnier, I am so grateful for your time and care: Beth Whitelaw, Grace Harrison, Francesca Eades, Leonie Lock, Marina Stavropoulou and Alex Kirby, as well as freelancers Rachael Beale and Michelle Bullock.

Thanks to Rob Greacen, Fiona Morrison and all the team at Stay Original for giving me time and space to write as Writer-in-Residence. Without you, I might have started this book, but I definitely wouldn't have finished it.

One of the catalysts for One Ukrainian Summer was an event – Translation Firebird – hosted by Cathy McAteer and Muireann Maguire at St Catherine's College, University of Cambridge, in April 2022. Thank you for the inspiration and the support.

Thanks to Yuliya Kostyuk at the University of Exeter who consulted on the Ukrainian and Russian in these pages, on the transliterations and on the translations, whilst being sensitive to the reality I wanted to reflect in the writing. We all make mistakes when we are learning a language, and this is a book about someone learning two languages and sometimes getting mixed up between them. Any errors or discrepancies are in spite of Yuliya's excellent work and are purely down to me.

A special mention to Olia Hercules and Alissa Timoshkina. Their #CookForUkraine project inspired me to realise that even if the darkest and most depressing of times, you can do something that brings light and joy – and you can use that impetus to raise funds for an urgent cause. For more on the legacy of their work, go to www.ukrainehub.uk.